Saga of the
DEVIL
and
GOD'S
LOVE
and Redemptive
PLAN
for Mankind

ROBERT L. SHEPHERD, JR.

ISBN 978-1-953223-20-3 (paperback)
ISBN 978-1-953223-22-7 (digital)

Rushmore Press LLC
1 800 460 9188
www.rushmorepress.com

Printed in the United States of America

DEDICATION

I dedicate this book to my wife of 37 years, the lovely and gifted Tammara (Ames) Shepherd. I also dedicate it to the one in whom I believe; my Lord and Savior Jesus Christ. And prayerfully I dedicate this book to everyone who read it. May you feel and experience the love of God and may His prosperity and grace eternally rest upon you.

CONTENTS

ACKNOWLEDGEMENT

I would like to acknowledge and thank my wife for spending her valuable time helping me with organizing and typing the manuscript to this work. But I would like to especially thank the late Reverend Elaine R. Westbrook who helped me with my books in the past as my editor and publisher. She was a darling saint and a great soul. I miss her dearly.

INTRODUCTION

Being a student of the Bible for most of my life I can clearly see prophecies from this grand old book are rapidly and daily being fulfilled. The Bible has proven to me to be accurate and indeed the infallible word of God. Only someone Omniscient could have predicted so many things that are now coming to past upon this planet earth.

I am convinced that there is a Creator (First Cause) and that there is a place called Heaven, where the good and Omnipotent Father of all creation reign.

On the other hand, I also believe that an evil creature call the devil exits. Satan already know that the Creator God has judged and appointed him and his coconspirator to hell and to the ETERNAL LAKE of FIRE; so to hurt the loving God, he is trying to take every boy, girl, man and woman he can with him to this place of torment.......... yes, hell is real.

After reading this book, you will know the whole story of the epic battle between good and evil. I pray and hope you'll choose the right side in this ancient war. This book will set before you life and death...... choose LIFE.

CHAPTER 1

EXPOSING THE DEVIL

Making known the Deceiver,
Tempter, Liar, Thief,
Accuser, Adversary, Destroyer
and Spiritual Enemy of man's Soul

THIS BOOK WAS given to me by the Holy Spirit to inform God's people and the world that there is a real devil.

Satan is deceptive. And he does not want the world and the Church of God to know that he exists so he comes incognito and hides himself behind the curtains, in the shadows, orchestrating and moving furniture and characters around on the gigantic stage of life—in his role as **chief stage conductor** or *"god of this world"*. If Satan keeps himself hid, he can more effectively perform his work. Therefore, he

1

has mastered (behind the curtains) the art of masking in the ***cloak of Anonymity***.

There are highly educated people, such as writers, doctors, professors, lawyers and scientists...and there are some common everyday folks that do not believe in the existence of a real devil. But believe me, my friend, Satan is real...**the devil does exist**. I am writing this book to make you aware of this fact. I will give you proof from the Word of God itself, that the devil is alive and well on planet earth. Some preachers or so-called men of the cloth, will tell you that Satan does not exit... ***Clog your ears...Run...And don't hear them!***

People of the earth, whether you believe it or not, the Devil is real. And he does not come wearing a red suit, dangling a long tail with horns on his head and a pitch folk in his hands...He's more subtle than that.

He comes in a phone call, a handshake or advice from a friend...or in the seductive smile of a neighbor. He comes in a thought or a suggestion. He comes in the comradeship of a peer. He comes with an offering of cake and candy...and with gold and silver. But be wise, my friend and do not accept his goods. For our Lord, Jesus Christ has informed us of his real motives... *The thief cometh not but for to steal and to kill and to destroy.*

The purpose of this book, **EXPOSING THE DEVIL**, is not to cause you to fear, or cause you to look for a devil behind every bush... It is to make you realize and become attentively aware that there are sinister forces on this planet that are trying to destroy you.

The *purpose* of this book is *to inform you* that there is help...You have hope.

About 2000 years ago, God sent his Son into the earth to suffer and die for the sins of man... If you accept him as your Lord and Savior, you can escape the diabolical plots and snares of the **Evil One**.

EXPOSING THE DEVIL will take you through the Word of God from **Genesis** to **Revelation** and will let you see Satan as he really is. As you read this book, you will not only **observe his rise**, but you will also witness *his fall*... You will learn how the Devil originated and you will watch and observe as you turn the pages; his predestined and tragic end.

You will also learn, by reading this book, the tactics and strategies Satan use to deceive the world and to immobilize and hinder the people of God....

A child of God does not have to live a mundane and defeated lifestyle. Jesus Christ has paid the price for each of his children to live a *life overflowing in abundance.*

As a child of God, *no weapon formed against you can prosper* when you *know who you are, believe God,* and *walk in the integrity of His Word.*

Not boasting in myself as co-author of this book, but giving all glory to God; I know of no other book that has, through the supernatural binoculars of God's Word, peeped into the invisible realms of heaven and hell and painted a more accurate portrait of the reality of Satan and his cohorts, as this book does.

Read this book prayerfully—with an opened heart. You will be blessed... and you will enjoy it!

Your friend in Christ,
Robert L. Shepherd Jr.
Evangelist of the Cross

WHO IS THE DEVIL AND WHERE DID HE COME FROM?

The devil is a defeated foe who has no power. He's a roaring lion who has no claws or teeth. The weapons he use to keep men in fear and in bondage are lies: false accusations of God's unfailing love for man; and false accusations of God's unfailing commitment and desire for man's deliverance and salvation.

The devil, belligerently-like, roars accusations of God being an austere God into the ears of men, so that men, even Believers, might fear and be reluctant to approach the Heavenly Father for help in time of trouble.

But we, as Believers, are the apples of God's eye. God loves us and He will fight for us. God also knows His children... and He chose us as **HIS**, even before the foundation of the world (**Ephesians 1:4**)

God knows our character, our makeup, our **body** and the very essence of our **spirit** and **soul**. And he has already taken care of all of our individual and physical needs in this earth and HE has given us all things *pertaining to life and godliness.*

God did not make a mistake when He chose and called you and me... *He will see us through this life and we will win.* We must trust Him...His thoughts and plan for us are *for good and not for evil.*

"For I know the thoughts that I think toward you, saith the Lord, thoughts of peace, and not of evil, to give you an expected end." **(Jeremiah 29:11)**

Everything believers encounter on their travel through this life, the rough roads and the low valleys, the dry deserts and the rugged wilderness, are ordained of God...Jesus has gone before us and HE has prepared our path by making every unbearable place bearable and every crooked place straight. *The way of the <u>righteous</u> or <u>good man</u> is ordered of the Lord...*

We will make it!!!

Fellow Wayfarer, if you must endure forty years in a desert of struggles and adversities, be confident, don't murmur or complain—keep the Faith...

God will see you through—just as He did the children of Israel on their wilderness journey.

Concerning the fiery trails, afflictions and tribulations we go through as Christians—no matter how intense, horrific, challenging or hopeless they appear; we must know that the Son of God has already entered the blazing furnace before us. He has tame the raging fire and prepared a way for our victory and escape... Our only role is to keep praying and keep looking to the cross of Christ...keep pleading **HIS Blood and trusting HIS word**.

You see, even before we entered our mothers' wombs, God knew us and preordained us, specifically for the work we must do in this life. *"Then the word of the Lord came unto me, saying, Before I formed thee in the belly I knew thee; and before thou camest forth out of the womb I sanctified thee, and I ordained thee a prophet unto the nations."* (**Jeremiah 1:5**)

Our lives are ordered by our All Knowing Father. *"The steps of a good man are ordered by the Lord: and he delighteth in his way."* (**Psalms 37:23**)

All things God's people encounter (both good and bad) work together for their ultimate good. **Everything** Saints encounter and endure is for a *divine purpose and for the glory of God.* You see, God is Sovereign and God is in control. Believe it or not, the devil works for God and the devil cannot do anything unless God approves or allows it. The evil the devil attempts against us, without God's permission, will always fail.

You might be now asking the question, "Do God congenially works as co-laborer; side-by-side with the devil?" **NO!** They are archenemies who only co-operate in their agendas concerning the affairs of men. Since God is Sovereign and Omniscient, His ultimate and predestined agenda will always prevail.

The devil is evil...His job or agenda is always <u>to steal</u>, <u>to kill</u> and <u>to destroy</u>. *"The thief cometh not, but for to steal, and to kill, and to destroy."* (**John 10:10a**)

God, on the other hand, is good. He sent His Son Jesus into the world that we might have **life**... *life more abundantly.* **God's agenda is to bless men.**

Christ came to give us *life more abundantly*, but we must desire and accept this life. We must repent of our sin and chose to live for HIM by accepting his love and forgiveness

7

for our sin and by partaking of the living water Christ freely gives.

"But whosoever drinketh of the water that I shall give him shall never thirst; but the water that I shall give him shall be in him a well of water springing up into everlasting life." (**John 4:14**)

"If any man thirst, let him come unto me, and drink. He that believeth on me, as the scripture hath said, out of his belly shall flow rivers of living water. (**John7:37b-38**).

"And the Spirit and the bride say, Come. And let him that heareth say, Come. And let him that is athrirst come. And whosoever will, let him take the water of life freely." (**Revelation22:17**)

God offers men Light and Living Water. He gives us His Word as a lamp unto our feet and as a light unto our pathway. And He supplies us with cool water to quench our thirst and refresh our weary souls.

As an alternative, the devil offers only darkness and death. He gives us poison to destroy our bodies and the bitter gall of sin to trouble our spirits and vex and destroy our souls.

Remember the Garden of Eden? God created man in His own image and placed him there. *"...male and female created Him them."* (**Genesis 1:27c**). Then God must have smiled on His creation: *"And God saw everything that He had made and behold it was very good..."* (**Genesis 1:31a**).

In the serene environment of Eden, where man ruled and was at peace; man would yet encounter a problem. You see, the devil was also lurking in the garden, disguised as a serpent. "*Now the serpent was more subtil than any beast of the field which the Lord God had made...*" (**Genesis 3:1a**)

The Old King James word, **subtil**, which we now spell **subtle** means: **1.** *Something slight and difficult to detect or analyze.* **2.** *Making or able to make fine distinctions, having acute perception.* **3.** *Ingenious, crafty.*

The Bible states that Satan was more subtle than any beast—this means that the devil is intelligent, ingenious, crafty... A being who is hard to detect or analyze (invisible or chameleon-like).

When the bible records "...*the serpent was more subtil than any beast of the field that the* <u>**Lord had made**</u>" we are directed to the fact that Satan is a created being...**Our Almighty God** made him.

You may now be thinking or asking yourself as you look around at all of the chaos, death and destruction this creature has wrought upon man and the earth. "Why would God create such a monstrosity—such an evil being?"

Let me answer your question... When God created Lucifer, he was beautiful and he was good. All that God creates is good. Lucifer, the *light bearer* or the *son of the morning*, became the devil on his own volition. He like man, had a choice... And he chose evil—even while daily dwelling and existing in the eternal presence of a good and loving God. **Sin** did not exist until Lucifer, out of a prideful heart, birthed **sin** into being. At one time, there was no sin or chaos in the whole universe...in heaven, on earth or beneath the earth. **Order** and **peace** ruled of the day.

Lucifer, God's chief archangel became the devil on his own accord. He had everything, but he was not satisfied... Instead of him being content in his role as chief musician, the covering cherub, and the pinnacle created being in the hierarchy of God's creatures, he wanted more. Thus, he allowed the deadly evils of pride, greed and envy, to fester and grow within his spirit and corrupt his heart.

Let's read his story: *"How art thou fallen from heaven, O Lucifer, son of the morning! How art thou cut down to the ground, which didst weaken the nations! For thou hast said in thine heart, I will ascend into heaven, I will exalt my throne above the stars of God; I will sit also upon the mount of the congregation in the sides of the north: I will ascend above the heights of the clouds; I will be like the most High."* (**Isaiah 14:12-14**)

The prophet Isaiah, when asking the devil the question, *"How did you fall from heaven?"* speaks of Lucifer as being the *"son of the morning"*. The American Standard Version translate this title for Lucifer as *"day star"*. This title lets us know that Lucifer was a pre-eminent angel of light before he became that sinister creature we now know as the devil. He's a dark sadistic angel now, but for purposes of deception, he still occasionally pretends to be an angel of light.

Isaiah goes on to give us the agenda of Lucifer—the dark and sinister plan of his evil heart which he (himself) had darkened when he allowed **pride**, **envy** and **greed** to inwardly fester, take root and grow.

Lucifer's Five "I's"

The first diabolic plan the prophet records that Lucifer birthed in his heart was this: "*I will ascend into heaven.*" So far, there was not a problem. You see, even though Lucifer walked the earth, he at that particular time had full access to the third heaven because he had not been kicked-out... He could come and go as he pleased. But even though Satan had now been kicked out of Heaven, he still can go there officially, in his role as the ***Accuser of the saints.***

Evil exalted itself and Lucifer crossed the line and became the devil when he proclaimed, "*I will exalt my throne above the stars of God*:

Now, there was a problem. The "stars" represent God's angelic hosts. When Lucifer made the statement that, he would exalt his throne above the "stars" He was saying that he would take over and control all of God's angelic beings, thus making himself Lord of Hosts. But even this was not enough for this **self-created evil one**. Next, he said, "*I will sit also upon the mount of the congregation, in the sides of the North*:"

The location **north** is up. In the bible it always represents the seat of God's power and the presence of God's throne. So what the devil was saying now, was this: "*I will exalt myself* to the sacred high place and sit on the throne of God."

What arrogance! What boldness! What foolishness! What was the devil thinking?

Here he was, *a trivial created being*, waging war to usurp the kingdom of a **Sovereign, Omnipotent, Eternal** and **Omnipresent God**—the Creator of all dominions and powers and worlds without end...

A God in whom all things, both invisible and visible, consist.

Still the devil was not through. Next he proclaimed, "*I will ascend above the heights of the cloud;*". The term "cloud" represents God's glory. So the devil's plan now was to take God's glory... His plan was "*to ascend above the heights of the clouds*" and obtain more glory than God, *his Creator.*

As though he hadn't done enough; his envy, greed and pride would now usher him into a world of total fantasy, insanity and make-belief... or did he really believe his next boast?

"*I will be like the most High.*"

This was the final straw!

Satan was now proclaiming himself to be God. So as quickly as this heavenly rebellion began, it ended.

God did not fight in this battle. God is a **Heavyweight**... And it would have not been fair for Him to fight against a **featherweight**. God simply spoke a word and observed as the evil angels and their boss Satan were cast from the third heaven by the archangel Michael and his warring angels.

Jesus informed his disciples in **Luke 10:18b**, "*...I beheld Satan as lightning fall from heaven.*"

John tells us in the book of **Revelation** concerning that old dragon (the devil): "*And his tail drew the third part of the stars of heaven, and did cast them to the earth...*" (**Revelation 12:4a**)

Somehow, through his charismatic personality and his "wiles", Satan persuaded one-third of the heavenly hosts to unite with him in this futile rebellion against God. Like Satan, these angels chose darkness and were banished and cast from the Third Heaven. Therefore, they will forever be separated from the warmth and protection of the Light of God's mercy, love and grace—they joined a losing team.

"And there was war in heaven: Michael and his angels fought against the dragon; and the dragon fought and his angels, And prevailed not; neither was their place found any more in heaven. And the great dragon was cast out, that old serpent, called the Devil, and Satan, which deceiveth the whole world: he was cast out into the earth, and his angels were cast out with him." (**Revelation 12:7-9**)

Judgment of the King and the Prince of Tyre

"The Word of the Lord came unto me, saying, Son of man, say unto the prince of Tyrus, Thus saith the Lord God; Because thine heart is lifted up, and thou hast saith, I am a God, I sit in the seat of God, in the midst of the seas; yet thou art a man, and not God, though thou set thine heart as the heart of God:" (**Ezekiel 28:1-2**)

In **Ezekiel chapter 28, verses 1-10,** the prophet addressed the **prince of *Tyrus*** (also pronounced ***Tyre***); the man who ruled and governed the region of **Tyre.**

The reason God was addressing the prince and the people of *this principality* was because of the ***arrogance of the*** *people*. These people had become lifted up in pride *in lieu* of their wealth and power and their supremacy to govern the seas—as sailors and merchants. In **verses 6** through **10**, God pronounced judgment against the **prince of Tyre**.

The people of this city were also being judged with their ruler because they had also rejected the Living God and had allowed Satan to rule them.

The prince of this city, because of his pride, had been deceived into thinking that he himself, was God—thus, allowing the false god Satan to possess and completely control him and govern the principality of Tyre through him.

The city of Tyre was not being controlled by one of Satan's subordinates...Tyre was being governed by the devil himself.

Through the prophet Ezekiel, God did not only address the prince and people of Tyre, He also addressed the devil who had arrogantly set up a stronghold and claimed territorial rights to the city.

In verses **1-10**, God addressed the man who ruled this city, **the prince of Tyre**...but in verses **11-19**, the prophet addressed the **devil** by referring to him as **the king of Tyre**. In God's pronouncement of judgment against the king of Tyre, we learn more about the character of the devil and about his ultimate fate... So let's read what God said about the **king of the principality of Tyre**—this creature we now know as **Satan:**

"Moreover the word of the Lord came unto me, saying, Son of man, take up a lamentation upon the king of Tyrus, and say

unto him, Thus saith the Lord God; Thou sealest up the sum, full of wisdom, and perfect in beauty. Thou hast been in Eden the garden of God; every precious stone was thy covering, the sardius, topaz and the diamond, the beryl, the onyx, the emerald, and the carbuncle, and gold, the workmanship of thy tabrets and of thy pipes was prepared in thee in the day that thou wast created. Thou are the anointed cherub that covereth; and I have set thee so; thou wast upon the holy mountain of God; thou hast walked up and down in the midst of the stones of fire. Thou wast perfect in thy ways from the day that thou wast created, till iniquity was found in thee. By the multitude of thy merchandise they have filled the midst of thee with violence, and thou hast sinned; therefore I will cast thee as profane out of the mountain of God; and I will destroy thee O covering cherub, from the midst of the stones of fire. Thine heart was lifted up because of thy beauty, thou hast corrupted thy wisdom by reason of thy brightness: I will lay thee before kings, that they may behold thee. Thou hast defiled thy sanctuaries by the multitude of thine iniquities, by the iniquity of thy traffic; therefore will I bring forth a fire from the midst of thee, I shall devour thee, and I will bring thee to ashes upon the earth in sight of all them that behold thee. All they that know thee among the people shall be astonished at thee; thou shalt be a terror, and never shalt thou be any more. **(Ezekiel 28:11-19)**

Let's examine the above text:

In **verse 12** the **KJV** term "*Thou sealest up the sum*" means that Lucifer, before he became the devil, *had it going on*.

The **NIV** reads like this, "*thou was the model of perfection.*"

This means that Lucifer was God's example of excellence. God created a masterpiece when he created **Lucifer**, t*he son of the morning.*

Verse 12 let us know that Lucifer was also wise and full of beauty. **Verse 13** records that Lucifer had access to the earth before he became the devil and that he had been in Eden, the garden of God.

When Lucifer was on earth in the Garden of Eden, he was arrayed with precious stones such as: diamonds, sapphires, emeralds, jasper and gold; to name a few. He also resonated with the joyous sound of music. Tabrets and pipes softly reverberated in him and though him as he angelically moved through the garden.

Verse 14 let us know that God created Lucifer and anointed him as a guardian cherub whose main duty was to cover and protect God's glory, as he strode up and down in the holy mountain of God's Kingly Chambers treading upon purifying holy stones of fire.

In **verse 15,** we learn that Lucifer was perfect in his ways from the day that God created him until sin was found in him... This sin was birthed and sprang forth when Lucifer allowed pride, envy and greed to fester and grow in his heart.

In **verse 16** of the **28th chapter** of **Ezekiel**, Lucifer allows the many gifts that God bestowed upon him to cause him to be puffed and *lifted up*... Lucifer then sin and rebels against God, his Creator. He is cast out of the third heaven— out of the mountain of God's glory and he loses his job as the covering cherub who threaded up and down in the midst of the stones of fire.

In **verse 17,** God says to Lucifer: *"Thine heart was lifted up because of thy beauty, thou hast corrupted thy wisdom by reason of thy brightness: I will cast thee to the ground, I will lay thee before kings, that they may behold thee."*

When Satan is cast down, God exhorts the heavens to rejoice and warns and admonishes the earth to mourn. *"Therefore rejoice, ye heavens, and ye that dwell in them. Woe to the inhabiters of the earth and of the sea: for the devil is come down unto you, having great wrath, because he knoweth that he hath but a short time."* (**Revelation 12:12**)

In **verses 18** and **19** of the **28th chapter** of **Ezekiel,** the devil terrorizes the nations of the earth until his reign is over. *"All they that know thee among the people shall be astonished at thee: Thou shalt be A terror, and never shalt thou be any more."* (**Ezekiel28:19**)

God informs us in **verse 19,** that the devil shall be a terror in the earth... but the good news God gives to the children of men, especially those who accept and trust in the redemptive work of His Son Jesus, is this: **Satan's terror will one day cease in the earth...and be no more.** *"...thou shalt be a terror, and never shalt thou be any more."*

Glory be to God!!!

Earlier in this chapter, I quoted from the prophet Isaiah as he recorded the story of the devil's pride and I told you of the five plans the **Evil One** *had conjured-up* to usurp God's kingdom. I quoted **Isaiah chapter 14, verses 12-14.**

Now, I will quote **verses15** and **16** of that **chapter**. "*Yet thou shalt be brought down to hell, to the sides of the pit. They that see thee shall narrowly look upon thee, and consider thee, saying, Is this the man that made the earth to tremble. That did shake kingdoms;*" (**Isaiah 14:15-16**).

In these verses God informed us how the devil would eventually be cast into hell, entrapped and surrounded by the walls of a bottomless pit. Isaiah also tells us that we will one day see the devil as this puny creature that sin has deformed and we will narrowly look at him. We will hardly notice or pay any attention to this being; until we are aware that he's the devil. Now, knowing his identity, we will take a second look at him and mentally ponder these questions: *Is this the creature that made the earth to tremble and shook nations? Is this the creature that caused all of that damage and wrecked all of that havoc in the earth? Is this the creature who destroyed and ruined so many lives? Is this the devil?* These are some of the questions we will ask ourselves as we see the devil for the very first time as he truly is... *not a creature to be feared, but a beast to pity*.

In the final chapter of this book, I will discuss in greater details *Satan's tragic and eternal fate*.

WHAT IS SATAN'S MISSION IN THE EARTH?

(And what are the tools he use to perform his task?)

In the book of **John, chapter 10** and **verse 10**, our Lord and Savior summed up the mission of Satan better than anyone could. Jesus said, *"The thief cometh not but for to steal, and to kill, and to destroy:"* (**John 10:10a**).

This statement lets us know that everything the devil does in the earth is for the downfall and destruction of the human race. The devil hates **mankind.** You see, the devil as chief fallen angel was already in the Garden of Eden when God spoke to Himself, the Spirit and the Word and said, *"Let us make man in our own image..."* (**Genesis 1:26a**).

Lucifer and the angels were not made in God's image. *So why would God form a creature from the dust of the earth to mold and shape in His own image*? This disturbed and annoyed the devil.

He was already angry with God for kicking him out of heaven, Now that God had created **man**, in His own Image, this birthed in Satan even more anger.

To add fuel to the fire of the devil's cauldron of bitterness and wrath, God goes on and say after he proclaimed to Himself that He would create a species called man and fashion in His own Image and likeness: And God added, *"...and let them have dominion over the fish of the sea, and over the fowl of the air and over the cattle, and over all the earth, and over every creeping thing that creepeth upon the earth."*

(**Genesis:1:26b**). *"Dominion over ever creeping thing that creepeth upon the earth?"* the snake pondered in his slithery mind... *"**That includes me**."*

So God knelled in the dust of the earth and out of earthly elements formed a man in his own image, and breathed spirit into this creature and produces for the very first time in the vast universe, *a living soul*.

This prideful creature, the devil, now has another master to deal with called...**man**. If he fought in heaven and would not willingly yield to God, his Creator, why would he now willingly *yield to* and *obey* **man;** a newly created being whom God had just created and assigned dominion and charge over all the earth.

NEVER! The devil proclaimed. So he immediately conjured up a plan and went to work: *"Now the serpent was more subtil than any beast of the field which the Lord God had made. And he said unto the woman, Yea, hath God said, Ye shall not eat of every tree of the garden? And the woman said unto the serpent, We may eat of the fruit of the trees of the garden: But of the tree which is in the midst of the garden God hath said, Ye shall not eat of it, neither shall ye touch it, lest ye die. And the serpent said unto the woman, ye shall not surely die. For God doth know that in the day ye eat thereof, then your eyes shall be opened, and ye shall be as gods, knowing good and evil And when the woman saw that the tree was good for food, and that it was pleasant to the eyes, and a tree to be desired to make* *one wise, she took of the fruit thereof, and did eat, and gave also unto her husband with her; and he did eat. And the eyes of them both were opened, and they knew that they were naked; and they sewed fig leaves together, and made themselves aprons."* (**Genesis 3:1-7**).

The Deceiver

Satan's pride would not allow him to sit silently by, as man entered the garden to reign in dominion and power—a garden which he had ruled and inhabited many years before man's entrance upon the scene. So in order to abort God's plan for man's dominion-ship of the earth, the devil would now use the tool of **deception** to trick man out of his birthright.

The serpent, being more subtle and wiling than any beast of the field that the LORD had made, was up for the task. Smoothly and snake-like, he approached the woman with the sole intent of deceiving and tricking her and Adam out of their Godly inheritance. In the book of **Galatians, chapter 6** and **verse 7**, God's Word reads, *"Be not deceived; God is not mocked: for whatsoever a man soweth, that shall he also reap."*

The **Master Deceiver** did not only deceive the human race but he also deceived himself. The god of this world blinded the eyes of Adam and Eve, but in doing so he also blinded and sucked himself into a *deeper miry pit* of captivity and darkness, *"...deceiving and being deceived."*

There's no hope for the devil. But for the men and women whom Satan has deceived, there is yet hope—*at the Cross of Christ*.

The blood of Christ can *cover, save men* and *restore* them back to God.

Jesus, our Messiah, stretches out his nail palmed hands inviting mankind... *"Come unto me, all ye that labour and are heavy laden, and I will give you rest, Take my yoke upon you, and learn of me; for I am meek and lowly in heart: and ye shall find rest unto your souls."* (**Matthew 11:28-29**)

The Tempter

There are only **three** areas in a man's life where the devil can tempt him. The Apostle John told us of those three areas: *"Love not the world, neither the things that are in the world, If any man love the world, the love of the Father is not in him. For all that is in the world, **the lust of the flesh** and **the lust of the eyes**, and **the pride of life**, is not of the Father, but is of the world."* (**I John 2:15-16**)

The devil tempted our Lord and Savior Jesus Christ in these three areas, but our Lord triumphantly passed every test. The Word of God lets us know that Jesus was tempted in every area, as all men are tempted, yet he did not sin. (**Hebrews 4:15**)

Luke chapter 4, verses 1 and 2 states: *"And Jesus being full of the Holy Ghost returned from Jordan, and was led by the Spirit into the wilderness, being forty days tempted of the devil.*

And in those days he did eat nothing: and when they were ended, he afterward hungered."

Immediately, after Jesus had been baptized in the river of Jordan by John the Baptist and the voice of God, The Father, proclaimed from heaven, *"This is my beloved Son, in whom I am well pleased"* Matthew records this: *"Then was Jesus led up of the Spirit into the wilderness to be tempted of the devil. And when he had fasted forty days and forty nights, he was afterward an hungred."* (**Matthew 4:1-2**)

Knowing that Jesus was fasting and had not eaten in forty days, the devil tempted Jesus first in the area where he knew our Savior was the most vulnerable: in the area of the flesh. *"And when the tempter came to him, he said, If thou be the Son of God, command that these stones be made bread."* (**Matthew 4:3**)

Satan wanted Jesus to hearken to his voice and turn desert stones into bread, in order to appease His hunger...and satisfy **the lust** (desire) **of the flesh.** But Jesus would not yield even being hungry. He held His ground and responded with the Word of God: *"... Man shall not live by bread alone, but by every word that proceedeth out of the mouth of God."* (**Matthew 4:4b**)

The devil next took Jesus to Jerusalem and placed Him on the pinnacle of the temple and tried to get Him to jump— to test the validity of God's Word.

"Then the devil taketh him up into the holy city, and setteth him on a pinnacle of the temple, And saith unto him, If thou be the Son of God, cast thyself down: for it is written, He shall give

his angels charge concerning thee: and in their hands they shall bear thee up, lest at any time thou dash thy foot against a stone." (**Matthew 4:5-6**)

This scripture the devil was referring to can be found in **Psalms 91:11-12**.

Jesus did not demonstrate to the devil that He was the Only Begotten Son of God or that He had favor with God and the heavenly hosts by casting himself down from the Temple. **Jesus knew who He was! ...** If Jesus had yielded to the voice of the enemy and endeavored to prove His Deity and the validity of God's Word by jumping headlong off the temple, He would have manifested the sin of **the pride of life.** Thus, Jesus responded saying: *"It is written again, Thou shalt not tempt the Lord thy God."* (**Matthew 4:7**)

Satan, in his haughtiness continued to **try** Jesus.

"Again, the devil taketh him up into an exceeding high mountain, and sheweth him all the kingdoms of the world, and the glory of them; And saith unto him, "All these things will I give thee, If thou will fall down and worship me." (**Matthew 4:8-9**)

The arrogance of the devil!!! The devil was showing Jesus all the riches and glory of the world, expecting Jesus to sell out to the sin of ***the lust of the eyes*** and fall to His knees to worship an inferior created-being whom **HE Himself** had created. (*read* **John chapter one, verses 1-3**).

What AUDACITY!!! What Gall!!! It was now time for the devil to go! *"Then saith Jesus unto him, Get thee hence, Satan: for it is written, Thou shalt worship the Lord thy God, and him only shalt thou serve."* (**Matthew 4:10**)

In the Garden of Eden, Adam and Eve faced the same temptations: **The lust of the flesh, the lust of the eyes** and **the pride of life**. Unfortunately for the human race, Adam and Eve yielded to all three.

Let us now go to **Genesis**, the book of beginnings. *"... And he said unto the woman, yea, hath God said, Ye shall not eat of every tree of the garden? And the woman said unto the serpent, We may eat of the fruit of the trees of the garden: But of the fruit of the tree which is in the midst of the garden God hath said, Ye shall not eat of it, neither shall ye touch it, lest ye die."* (**Genesis 3:1b-3**)

The devil was appealing to Eve's fleshly appetite and desire when he presented the luscious fruit. He was inviting her to yield to the lust of the flesh and to blatantly disobey and dishonor God by partaking of it...and she Bit. Adam would also take the bait.

Next, the devil appealed to **the lust of the eyes** to seduce Adam and Eve. *"And when the woman saw that the tree was good for food, and that it was pleasant to the eyes..."* (**Genesis 3:6a**)

Just as the devil had shown Jesus all the glory and beauty of the world and invited him to yield so that He might attain them, the devil was now offering man this beautiful forbidden fruit to visualize, to lust after and to partake of.

Jesus overcame the Tempter, when He was confronted in this area, by resorting to and obeying the Word of God. But Adam and Eve did not...Somehow, they momentarily forgot the words that God had spoken to them and they yielded to the temptation of **the lust of the eyes** also.

Adam and Eve yet had a way to escape but they would now yield to the most destructive and deadliest sin of them all: **the pride of life.** Listen to what the devil tells them: *"For God doth know that in the day ye eat thereof, then your eyes shall be opened, and ye shall be as gods, knowing good and evil."* **(Genesis 3:5)**

"And when the woman saw that the tree was good for food and that it was pleasant to the eyes and a tree to be desired to make one wise, she took of the fruit thereof, and did eat, and gave also unto her husband with her; and he did eat." **(Genesis 3:6)**

All ungodly quests for **respect, recognition, knowledge, wisdom, fame** and **power** is **PRIDE.**

Satan had now tempted man and deceived man...and usurped him of his authority in the earth. Man got a raw deal. The fruit of **the Tree of knowledge of Good and Evil** only contributed to mankind the *evil nature* and knowledge of Satan. Man already had the **Knowledge of Good.** He already knew **GOOD** and he was already *very good. "And God saw everything that he had made, and behold it was very good."* **(Genesis 1:31a)**

Man was already like God. After all, he had been created in the likeness and image of the **CREATOR**... his Good, Wise, Loving and Compassionate Father.

Man was tempted with the proverbial apple by the Master Tempter and he bit.

Temptation is the most popular device Satan uses to bait men. He offers **man** everything and gives him nothing but *death and destruction*. **James tells** us this: *"Let no man say when he is tempted, I am tempted of God: for God cannot be tempted with evil, neither tempteth he any man: But every man is tempted when he is drawn away of his own lust, and enticed. Then when lust hath conceived, it bringeth forth sin: and sin, when it is finished, bringeth forth death."* (**James 1:13-15**)

The Liar

"And the serpent said unto the woman, Ye shall not surely die:" (**Genesis 3:4**)

Magicians deceive their audience with gadgets and slight of hand tricks. The magicians will have you focus on one thing, the left hand for instance—to keep you from observing the things they are actually doing with the right hand.

So it is with Satan... But he does not use hand tricks and rigged-up gadgets. Satan uses lies to deceive men and women. He came to Adam and Eve with a smile, offering them *enlightenment* and *advancement to another level— so to speak*. But the level the devil was trying to get them to take was not an upward-mobility one...*it was a downward plunge*.

Like it was unwise to accept the gift of the Trojan Horse, man's acceptance of the words of Satan was foolish and unwise. This mistake would not only allow the devil and his cohorts entrance into a city—it would give the devil and his demons access to a whole planet; to enter it and contaminate it with plagues, chaos, and destruction and death.

In **Genesis chapter 2, verses 16** and **17**, God specifically warns man that by partaking of the fruit of the tree of the knowledge of good and evil, he would *surely die...* and God cannot lie. God told man that "...*every tree of the garden thou mayest freely eat:*" Only one tree was forbidden man by God, not to eat of. But The devil told Adam and Eve in **Genesis 3:4b-5** "..*Ye shall not surely die: For God doth know that in the day ye eat thereof, then your eyes shall be opened, and ye shall be as gods, knowing good and evil.*" Satan implies that God is not being totally honest with Adam and Eve—that God is holding back on them, so to speak and that HE is impeding their growth.

That **Liar**, the **devil**! The father of lies tells Adam and Eve, "Thou shalt not surely die" and they believed him.

Just like the devil lied to the first man and woman, he's lying to men and women today. Jesus has told us that there is only one way to God and that way is through Him. Yet men and women, deceived and blinded by the god of this world, are seeking other ways to God. Solomon tells us in **Proverbs 14:12**: "*There is a way which seemeth right unto a man, but the end thereof are the ways of death.:* He also warns us in **Proverbs 30:5-6**: "*Every word of God is pure: he is a shield unto them that put their trust in him. Add thou not unto his words, lest he reprove thee, and thou be found a **liar**.*"

Readers, I must inform you today from the word of God that: "***The wages of sin is death.***"... Only through Christ is there forgiveness of sin and eternal life. So **P-l-e-a-s-e—Don't listen to Satan...He's a Liar**.

In **Revelation chapter 21** and **verse 8**, the Word informs us that "*all liars*" shall have their part in the Lake that burneth with fire and brimstone... The **Master Liar, Satan,** will be there. His spot there has been *specially reserved* by God Himself.

The Thief

"*Then said Jesus unto them again, Verily, verily, I say unto you, I am the door of the sheep. All that ever came before me are thieves and robbers: but the sheep did not hear them. I am the door: by me if any man enter in, he shall be saved, and shall go in and out, and find pasture. The **thief** cometh not, but for to steal, and to kill, and to destroy: I am come that they might have life, and that they might have it more abundantly.*" (**John 10:7-10**)

The ultimate objective of the Master Thief, that old serpent the devil, is to use deceit, temptation and diabolical lies to bereft mankind of the redemptive grace and abundant life for which the Son of God sacrificially gave His life for men to freely receive.

There is only one door and one way into the Kingdom of God... and that Door is **JESUS**. But the Master Thief has sent his thieves and robbers (wolves in sheep clothing) into the earth with fake doors; offering entrance into **LIFE**... but those doors—**everyone**—leads to **Death**.

There is only one name under heaven, given among men whereby we must be saved; and that name is **JESUS!** Jesus has already told us the mission of the thief: The thief cometh not but for to steal and to kill and to destroy. He comes to steal the hearts of men, kill the bodies of men and destroy men' souls of eternal life and hope. That is why Jesus told us to: *"Lay not up for yourselves treasures upon earth, where moth and rust doth corrupt, and where thieves break through and steal: But lay up for yourselves treasures in heaven, where neither moth nor rust doth corrupt, and where thieves do not break through nor steal: For where your treasure is, there will your heart be also."* (**Matthew 6:19-21**)

"Men do not despise a thief, if he steal to satisfy his soul when he is hungry; But if he be found, he shall restore sevenfold; he shall give all the substance of his house." (**Proverb 6:30-31**). The Master Thief, in order to satisfy his envy, pride, greed and the emptiness of his spirit, stolen from us... But he has been caught. If you're reading this book today, I am exposing him to you...

The devil took your stuff! Don't despise him...Just take back your stuff!

If you're a Believer, the laws of God are on your side. Take that crook to court. In the courtroom of Heaven, your Advocate, Christ Jesus, will plead your case and you'll get back, sevenfold, your stolen goods.

Just ask in faith...***and demand your stuff back!***

If the thief has stolen your health...Demand it back! If he has taken your children or spouse...Demand them back! If he has stolen your money, your vehicle, your house or land...Demand it back. Demand it back in the Name of Jesus!

Denounce the devil and take back your stuff!

David Did!

While David and his men were at war fighting for the Philistines, the Amalekites entered their city, Ziglag, and burned it to the ground. The Amalekites took all of their property and precious goods, including their wives and children.

"And David *inquired of the Lord, saying, Shall I pursue after this troop? Shall I overtake them? And he answered him, Pursue: for thou shalt surely overtake them, and without fail recover all.*" (**I Samuel 30:8**)

When David and his men discovered whom the thieves were that took their stuff, they pursued them, confronted them and took back their stuff. "*And David recovered all that the Amalekites had carried away: And David rescued his two wives. And there was nothing lacking to them, neither small nor great, neither sons nor daughters, neither spoil, nor any thing that they had taken to them: David recovered all.*" (**I Samuel 30:18-19**). Not only did David and his men recover the things that the enemy had stolen from them—to enhance their possessions, they also took the enemy's stuff.

Attention! Attention!
Public announcement to the Readers
of this Book: "The Thief has been found!"
and his name is Satan.

If you are not saved, come to the cross of Christ, repent of your sins today and invite Jesus to be your Lord and Savior. Then with boldness, ask the **Supreme Judge** of the universe to make the Thief give back our stuff. In the **NAME OF JESUS**....*take back your stuff!!!*

The Accuser

"And I heard a loud voice saying in heaven, Now is come salvation, and strength, and the kingdom of our God, and the power of his Christ: for the accuser of our brethren is cast down, which accuses them before our God day and night." (**Revelation 12:10**)

"Then he showed me Joshua the high priest standing before the angel of the Lord and Satan standing at his right side to accuse him. The Lord said to Satan, 'The Lord rebuke you Satan! The Lord, who has chosen Jerusalem rebuke you!' Now Joshua was dressed in filthy clothes as he stood before the angel. The angel said to those who were standing before him, 'Take off his filthy clothes.' Then he said to Joshua, *"See, I have taken away your sin, and I will put rich garments on you."'* (**Zachariah 3:1-4**) NIV.

In this vision that God gives His prophet, Zachariah, he sees the high priest of God's people standing before the throne of God. And the devil, serving as prosecutor, is standing on Joshua's right side accusing him of having on unclean garments in the presence of a Holy Judge.

Joshua is in trouble...

But Look! The angel of the Lord is also standing there, *in Joshua's defense.*

So in response to the angel of the Lord, God says unto Satan, "*The Lord rebuke you, Satan! The Lord, who has chosen Jerusalem rebuke you! Is not this man a burning stick snatched from the fire?*" Our Lord rebukes the devil, informing him that HE called and chose Joshua as high priest. The Lord goes on to say that He, Himself, snatched Joshua from the ravishing fire of hell and damnation—just as a man would rapidly snatch a precious stick from a burning fire to keep it from being consumed...

Joshua belonged to God... One of the reason God could legally rescue Joshua from the fire is because the high priest stood before the angel of the Lord with the **sacrificial-substitutional blood** of the Lamb of God. Joshua, though clothed in filthy garments, was covered by *the Blood.* Therefore, the **angel of the Lord**, who was undoubtedly Jesus, the **Son of God**, said to the bailiff angels who were standing before Joshua: "*Take off his filthy clothes.*"

Then the angel of the Lord said, "*See, I have taken away your sin, and I will put rich garments on you.*" The angel of the Lord that Zechariah beheld was the Advocate and High Priest of heaven, Jesus Christ our Lord. For no one can forgive sin and adorn a filthy man in clean garments but our Savior and Lord. God says in His Word, "*Accuse not a servant unto* *his master, lest he (*the master*) curse thee, and thou be found guilty.*" (**Proverbs 30:10**)

Your Master Accuser, Satan, has been **rebuked**, **cursed** and **found guilty** by God. Therefore, do not allow his accusations to paralyze you and steal your hope.

If you are guilty of sin, ***repent, renounce your sins*** and ***plead the Blood.***

Like David, cry out: "*Have mercy upon me, O God, according to thy loving kindness: according unto the multitude of thy tender mercies blot out my transgressions. Wash me thoroughly from mine iniquity, and cleanse me from my sin. For I acknowledge my transgression: and my sin is ever before me. Against thee only have I sinned, and done this evil in thy sight: that thou mightest be justified when thou speakest, and be clear when thou Judgest. Behold, I was shapen in iniquity; and in sin did my mother conceive me. Behold, thou desirest truth in the inward parts: and in the hidden part thou shalt make me to know wisdom. Purge me with hyssop, and I shall be clean: wash me, and I shall be whiter than snow. Make me to hear joy and gladness; that the bones which thou hast broken may rejoice. Hide thy face from my sins, and blot out all mine iniquities. Create in me a clean heart, O God; and renew a right spirit within me. Cast me not away from thy presence; and take not thy Holy Spirit from me. Restore unto me the joy of thy salvation; and uphold me with thy free Spirit.*" (**Psalms 51:1-12**)

The Adversary

"Be sober, be vigilant; because your adversary the devil, as a roaring lion, walketh about, seeking whom he may devour: Whom resist steadfast in the faith, knowing that the same afflictions are accomplish in your brethren that are in the world." (**I Peter 5:8-9**)

The Apostle Peter; the same disciple who denied the Lord **3** times on the night of Christ's trial with the Sanhedrin Court, admonishes us to be sober and vigilant because there's an unseen adversary walking about as a roaring lion, seeking whom he may devour.

Peter was familiar with this adversary.

This adversary had caused him to lie and this adversary had even caused Peter to rebuke his Lord when Jesus began *"... to shew unto his disciples, how that he must go unto Jerusalem and suffer many things of the elders and chief priests and scribes, and be killed. And be raised again the third day."* (**Matthew 16:21**)

"Then Peter took him, (Jesus) and began to rebuke him, saying, Be it far from thee, Lord: this shall not be unto thee." (**Matthew 16:22**)

"But he (Jesus) turned, and said unto Peter, Get thee behind me Satan: thou art an offense unto me: For thou savourest not the things that be of God, but those that be of men. (**Matthew 16:23**)

The Lord was not just rebuking Peter, He was also rebuking the devil who was trying to discourage and detour Him from His journey to the cross. Jesus addressed His adversary the devil and said to him, *"Get behind me Satan:..."* Jesus then turned to Peter and revealed to Peter the desire of his heart: *"For thou savourest not the things that be of God, but those that be of men."*

Jesus was familiar with this adversary that was battling Peter's soul because Jesus had dealt, victoriously with him many times before.

In **Luke 22:31**, Jesus told Peter who this adversary was and informed Peter of the adversary's plan for his life. Jesus says to Peter, his disciple: *"Behold, Satan hath desired to have you, that he may sift you as wheat: But I have prayed for thee, that thy faith fail not: and when thou art converted, strengthen thy brethren."*

Jesus did not rebuke the adversary in **Luke 22:31.** Nor did He pray that the devil leave Peter alone. Jesus simply prayed that His disciple's faith would not fail and that Peter—once he was strengthened—would strengthen others.

Subsequently, when Peter tells the church in his epistle to be sober and vigilant because there was a roaring lion lurking in the shadows, waiting for a stranded, wounded or slumbering sheep to cross its path so that it might silently swoop down upon and devour…Peter was in essence, warning his brethren of the adversary and strengthening his brothers and sisters in their faith.

In Jesus' prayer for Peter, Jesus did not pray that Peter would live completely free from the wiles, schemes and harassment of the devil.

From past experience, Peter had learned that no one who is truly called and chosen of God could live a life free of satanic harassment. Did not David say, *"Many are the afflictions of the righteous: but the Lord delivereth him out of them all.*"? (**Psalm 34:19**)

Paul told his son in the gospel, Timotheus, "*But thou hast fully known my doctrine, manner of life, purpose, faith, longsuffering, charity; patience, persecutions, afflictions which came unto me at Antioch and Iconium, at Lystra; what persecutions I endured: but out of them all the Lord delivered me. Yea, and all that will live godly in Christ Jesus shall suffer persecution.*". (**I Timothy 3:10-12**)

Jesus informed his disciples: "*Behold, the hour cometh, yea, is now come, that ye shall be scattered, every man to his own, and shall leave me alone: and yet I am not alone because the Father is with me. These things I have spoken unto you, that in me ye might have peace. In the world ye shall have tribulation: but be of good cheer; I have overcome the world.*" (**John 16:23-33**)

Peter had learned that the church of God was an army and that saints would have to watch, pray, fight and "*endure hardness as good soldiers.*" Even though as followers of Christ, our battles and tribulations will be many... we must have confidence and be assured that through every struggle, we'll come forth *more than conquerors through Christ who love us and gave his life for us!*

We can be of good cheer because we're Overcomers of this world. Our Lord and Savior overcame the world— we'll overcome it too.

The Lord Himself tells us: "*Blessed are ye, when men shall revile you, and persecute you, and shall say all manner of evil against you falsely, for my sake. Rejoice and be exceeding* glad: *for great is your reward in heaven: for so persecuted they the prophets which were before you."* (**Matthew 5:11-12**)

Peter tells us to resist our adversary and be steadfast in the faith, recognizing we are not alone and that others have also fought and are fighting this good fight of faith. He admonishes us to hold on and Peter exhorts...***It will get better.***

"But the God of all grace" he encourages us, *"who hath called us into his eternal glory by Christ Jesus, after that ye have suffered a while, make you perfect, stablish, strengthen, settle you."* (**I Peter 5:10**)

In the book of **Ephesians**, the **sixth chapter, verses 10** through **12**, Paul addresses the faithful at Ephesus with these words: *"Finally, my brethren, be strong in the Lord, and in the power of his might, Put on the whole Armour of God, that ye may be able to stand against the wiles of the devil. For we wrestle not against flesh and blood, but against principalities, against powers, against the rulers of the darkness of this world, against spiritual wickedness in high places."*

Whereas Peter tells us to be sober and vigilant (sound of mind and alert) in our warfare against our adversary, the devil—Paul, on the other hand, admonishes us to always wear our armor and *"...to be strong in the Lord, and in the power of his might.:"*

Peter tells us to be alert and watchful of the roaring lion, Satan. But Paul lets us know that, beside Satan, there are other adversaries...the lion is not alone.

We are not fighting against *flesh and blood,* Paul advises us. Our warfare is with **unseen forces in the heavens**...satanic princes headquartered in the air.

Like a good fire-star General who is familiar with the forces, strategies and tactics of the enemy, Paul let us know exactly who we're fighting. My country, the United States of America, has five major branches of Armed Services: The Army, the Navy, the Air Force, the Marines and the coast Guard. Within each Branch there are Special Forces who are highly and specifically trained and assigned to perform certain individual tasks. In each Armed Branch of the service there is an echelon—or chain of command. For instance, in our Army, the top of the echelon consists of the generals and the bottom of the echelon consists of the privates.

The United States president, who is the Commander and Chief, is the head of all of our military branches, and he obeys no one in the chain of command, because he is the head.

However, the privates in the Army have many in rank above them whom they must submit to and obey.

Just as the Nations of this earth organizes their military branches in order for things to function effectively and efficiently...so does Satan. His echelonic hierarchy from top to bottom consists of **Principalities, Powers, Rulers of Darkness**, which is followed by **Spiritual Wickedness in high places.** These evil forces are not only in an echelonic order...they are also classified in branches.

I know it has been taught that some of these four branches of evil mentioned in **Ephesian**, consist of people. But that is not so.

Yes, Satan has men and women in his army but this list that Paul gives us, do not include them. None of these branches of satanic warriors mentioned in the **sixth chapter** of **Ephesians** consist of human beings.

Paul, when categorizing these sinister forces, specifically tells us that they are not flesh and blood or humans. Before naming them Paul stretches the fact: "...*we wrestle not against flesh and blood*..." And then he goes on to give the list.

But I would like to inform you that in some nations, cities and municipalities, there are also human beings serving the devil under the official titles of principalities, powers, rulers of darkness and spiritual wickedness in high places— serving directly under the leadership and control of their satanic counterparts in the heavenlies.

No! I am not saying that every politician has a devil or is personally possessed by the devil like the prince of Tyre was—whom we read about in the first chapter of this book... The principalities, powers, rulers of darkness and spiritual wickedness in high places that control certain regions of the earth could be working, not necessarily through the political leader, but they could be working through the rich man on the hill or even through the old poor woman living in the rundown shanty in the ghetto...or through both.

Enough bad news! Let me give you some encouraging news: the praises and effectual fervent prayer of the righteous

can and **will** always prevail over devilish forces and uproot and pull-down spiritual strongholds.

Though men are in a life and death struggle with these sinister beings, we must not fear or be intimidated by our diabolic adversaries. For the Word of God encourages us with these words: *"He will keep the feet of his saints, and the wicked shall be silent in darkness; for by strength shall no man prevail. The adversaries of the Lord shall be broken to pieces; out of heaven he thunder upon them: the Lord shall judge the ends of the earth; and he shall give strength unto his king, and exhalt the horn of his anointed."* (**I Samuel2:9, 10**)

When Samuel quotes, *"...he shall give strength unto his king, and exhalt the horn of his anointed"*, the Prophet is foretelling the coming in glory and power of our Commander and Chief—our Savior and Warrior, the Lord Jesus Christ!

"Behold," God promises Moses, *"I send an Angel before thee, to keep thee in the way, and to bring thee into the place which I have prepared. Beware of him, and obey his voice, provoke him not; for he will not pardon your transgression: for my name is in him. But if thou shalt indeed obey his voice, and do all that I speak; then I will be an enemy unto thine enemies, and an adversary unto thine adversaries."* (**Exodus 23:20-22**)

The Destroyer

"The thief cometh not, but for to steal, and to kill, and to destroy." Everything Satan touches he destroys. It's his nature. Avoid him at all cost. Put your family under the covering

of the Blood of Christ... And through prayer, mark your doorposts with this crimson hope—so whenever the **angel of death and destruction** comes nigh your dwellings and knocks at your door to summon your sons and daughters; the blood will chase him off... and you and your family will live.

In imitation of David the Psalmist, we should always cry out unto our God when the destroyer comes to us to sink our soul into the waters and quicksand of despair and flood our eyes with rivers of tears: "*Save me, O God; for the waters are come in unto my soul. I stand in deep mire, where there is no standing: I am come into deep waters, where the floods overflow me. I am weary of my crying: my throat is dried: mine eyes fail while I wait for my God. They that hate me without a cause are more than the hairs of mine head: they that would destroy me, being mine enemies wrongfully, are mighty...*" (**Psalms 69:1-4**)

My brother or sister, when the **Destroyer** knocks at your door (and believe me, he will) don't panic or fear. **Raise your head!!! Dry your eyes.** And tell **JESUS** on that old bully, the **Destroyer**... And watch Him fight for you!

"*Then they cry unto the Lord in their trouble, and he saveth them out of heir distresses. He send his word, and healed them, and delivered them from their destruction.*" (**Psalms 107:19-20**)

Know this Saints of God: <u>God will deliver us from the sword of the **Destroyer**</u>. The Prophet Isaiah encourages us: "*In righteousness shalt thou be established: thou shalt be far from oppression; for thou shalt not fear: and from terror; for it shall not come near thee. Behold, they shall surely gather together, but not by me: whosoever shall gather together against thee shall fall* *for thy sake. Behold, I have created the smith that bloweth the coals in the fire, and that bringeth forth an instrument for his work; and I have created the* **waster to destroy.** *No weapon that is formed against thee shall prosper; and every tongue that shall rise against thee in judgment thou shalt condemn. This is the heritage of the servants of the Lord, and their righteousness is of me, saith the Lord."* (**Isaiah 54:14-17**)

WHAT IS SATAN'S FATE

Satan has already been convicted—proven and found guilty and he knows that his time is short. He's out on his own recognizance, for now, but he is facing an irrevocable and pending fate. The day for him to be shackled, handcuffed, arrested and taken into custody, accordingly; so he can start serving his eternal sentence, is rapidly approaching and is *at hand*. However, before Satan's reign as **Chief World Terrorist** is over, many things must yet come to pass. Paul tells Timothy, *"This know also, that in the last days perilous times shall come, For men shall be lovers of their own selves, covetous, boasters, proud, blasphemers, disobedient to parents, unthankful, unholy, Without natural affection, trucebreakers, false accusers, incontinent, fierce, despisers of those that are good, Traitors, heady, highminded, lovers of pleasures more than lovers of God: Having a form of godliness, but denying the power thereof."* **(II Timothy 3:1-5a)**

You do not have to be a great observer like Sherlock Holmes to realize perilous times are here. Just watch your television...Watching the evening news will let one know that men are lovers of themselves—self-centered and selfish; and that men are haters and blasphemers of God.

Many men and women are greedy, boastful and proud. And their children are disobedient, unthankful, ungrateful and unholy... Mothers and fathers, lacking natural affection, are unloving and un-nurturing toward their children. They are liars, promise breakers and untrustworthy. There are many men and women who are lascivious, fierce, arrogant, troublemakers and despisers of those that are good.

Same-sex marriages among women and men are not just being tolerated in today's society, but these abominable-unions are being sanctioned, endorsed and protected by state and federal laws. Man's love for pleasure is greater than his love for God... He talks about God but he will not believe or walk in the power that only the true and living God (our Lord and Savior Jesus Christ) provides and delivers.

In the book of **Matthew, chapter 24, Jesus** told of other events that would take place in the end times. Let's read **verse 3** through **14:** *"And as he sat upon the mount of Olives, the disciples came unto him privately, saying, Tell us, when shall these things be? And what shall be the sign of thy coming, and of the end of the world? And Jesus answered and said unto them, Take heed that no man deceive you. For many shall come in my name, saying, I am Christ; and shall deceive many. And ye shall hear of wars and rumours of wars: see that ye be not troubled: for all these things must come to pass, but the end is not yet. For nation shall rise against nation, and kingdom against kingdom: and there shall be famines, and pestilences, and earthquakes, in divers places. All these are the beginning of sorrows. Then shalt they deliver you up to be afflicted, and shall kill you: and ye shall be hated of all nations for my name's sake. And then shall many be offended, and shall betray one another, and shall hate one another. And many false prophets shall rise, and shall deceive* *many. And because iniquity shall abound, the love of many shall wax cold.*

But he that shall endure unto the end, the same shall be saved. And this gospel of the kingdom shall be preached in all the world for a witness unto all nations; and then shall the end come."

In the text above, Jesus told his disciples of things people in the end times would see and encounter. And we are presently experiencing all of these things. As I write, wars are raging in the Middle East, South America, Indonesia and in other parts of the world. Women, children and men are starving and begging for bread in Africa, North Korea, India, Mexico and even in the streets and slums of America.

On every continent, people of God are being persecuted. In some parts of Africa—women, men and children are been raped, thrown alive into burning fires and hacked into pieces with machetes because they will not renounce their faith and love for Christ. In Afghanistan, Indonesia, and numerous of other places, Christian are being imprisoned and some are even being shot to death or beheaded for the *gospel sake.*

Churches all over the world are being set ablaze and burnt to the ground because of people's hatred for the things of God.

In some public arenas of America, even in our government and also in some of our churches; *in the name of the god of* **Political Correctness**, preachers and chaplains are being forbidden and not allowed to pray in the **Name of Jesus.**

The pestilence of AIDS, the Ebola virus, bird flu, mad cow disease and other infectious viruses and germs are rapidly claiming victims. Tsunamis, hurricanes and volcanoes are blowing, raging and erupting in many places and earthquakes are shaking and swallowing and terrorizing the earth at an intensity and level not previously known in the history of mankind.

These diverse disasters are destroying lives and threatening to tumble and bankrupt entire nations.

As hurricanes drown the coastal regions of my country with rain, and blow and wash away homes and lives; in the central part of America, tornadoes are hurling from the skies, picking up and scattering the dreams, destiny and hopes of entire families as wildfires rage in the western states, wiping out houses and consuming venerable trees which have stood firm and Titan-like above our fertile plains for hundreds of years.

Industrial pollution and smog is contaminating our air. And the phenomenon of **Global change** is gradually being realized as our natural forest, exotic wild life and Majestic ice peaks are melting and vanishing from the face of the earth.

Designer drugs, crack and powder cocaine, crystal meth, heroin, alcohol, inhalants and prescription drugs are *capturing and hooking* the old and the young alike, entrapping them zombie-like in prisons of addiction and death.

This is happening on a lever never witnessed before in the history of the world.

And our preteen and teen boys and girls are joining gangs, killing one another and abusing and disrespecting their young bodies with drugs and promiscuous-premarital sex.

The conscienceless-immoral-steel-surgical-tyrant, surname **Legal Abortion**, is snatching millions of babies from the womb; snuffing out these little lives before they have a chance to enter the earth, and to grow-up and make their impact on our society.

Because iniquity abounds, our prisons are overcrowded... Therefore, new prisons are constantly being built to house more thieves, more gang-bangers, more drug dealers, more drug users, more drunk drivers, more extortionists, more psychopaths, more pedophiles, more prostitutes, more robbers and killers; as the incarceration numbers continue to escalate.

Mothers and fathers are killing and abandoning their children......And children are entering their parents' bedrooms and killing them in their sleep. Because iniquity abounds, the love of many has waxed cold.

Many occults and false religions are spreading throughout our world...

Men and women, like **Bar Jesus**, are proclaiming themselves to be gods or some great one.

Even though these evil things must occur and are occurring, the gospel (good news) is being preached in all the world for a witness unto all nations through satellite television, dvd's, books, magazines, pamphlets, videos, audio tapes and traveling evangelists...

The end is at hand.

In **chapter 2** of this book, we spoke of the fall of man in the Garden of Eden.

Let's now go back to **Genesis** and see what happened to the devil...

After the serpent deceived Adam and Eve and they had blatantly adhered to him, God killed and sacrificed the first living creature as a substitution-al blood-offering and covering—in order to take away the sin, fear, shame and spiritual death that came upon Adam and Eve for the obstinate and treasonous act they foolishly committed against their Creator. **(Genesis 3:21)**

Upon committing this sinister act, this couple self-reliantly attempted to cover themselves with fig leaves. But a greater covering... a blood sacrifice was needed.

The book of **Hebrews** lets us know that without the shedding of blood there is no remission of sin.

Therefore, in order for Adam and Eve's sin to be *covered* or *atoned for,* **something** or **Someone** had to die...

But there would be no atonement for the serpent. His destruction was sealed and foretold in **Genesis chapter 3, verses** 14 and **15.** *"And the Lord God said unto the serpent, Because thou hast done this, you art cursed above all cattle, and above every beast of the field; upon thy belly shalt thou go, and dust shalt thou eat all the days of thy life: And I will put enmity between thee and the woman, and between thy seed and her seed; it shall bruise thy head, and thou shalt bruise his heel."*

Isaiah 7:14 reads, "*Therefore the Lord himself shall give you a sign; Behold a virgin shall conceive, and bear a son, and shall call his name Immanuel* (God with us)."

When man sinned, God immediately set His plan into motion for the revival and restoration of mankind and for the doom and destruction of the devil. God told the serpent that there would be warfare between him and the Seed of the woman; and that in this warfare there would be a mortal blow: The woman Seed's **foot** would crush the head of the serpent. And in so doing, the Seed of the woman would suffer a bruised heel. Isaiah also prophesied, and it came to past, that through the womb of a virgin; the Son of God would enter the earth and dwell among men... And in due time, the Son would give his life so that many might live. "*...the Son of man came not to be ministered unto, but to minister, and to give his life a ransom for many.*" (**Mark 10:45**) By the wounding and bruising of Christ's heel—Christ physical suffering and death on the cross; our Lord destroyed the works of the devil and set men free from grief, sorrows, transgression, iniquities, sickness and death. **Isaiah** prophesied: "*Who hath believed our report: and to whom is the arm of the Lord revealed? For he shall grow up before him as a tender plant, and as a root out of a dry ground: he hath no form nor comeliness; and when we shall see him, there is no beauty that we should desire him. He is despised and rejected of men; a man of sorrows, and acquainted with grief: and we hid as it were our faces from him; he was despised, and we esteemed him not. Surely he hath borne our griefs, and carried our sorrows: yet we did esteem him stricken, smitten of God, and afflicted. But* *he was wounded for our transgressions, he was bruised for our iniquities: the chastisement of our peace was upon him; and with his stripes we are healed. All we like sheep have gone astray; we have turned every one to his own way; and the Lord hath laid on him the iniquity of us all."* **(Isaiah 53:1-6)**

When the devil heard directly from the mouth of God in **Genesis 3:14-15**, of the Coming Seed that would bruise his head, the devil initiated his own program to stop and counteract the plan of God.

First, he tried to contaminate the seed of the woman of promise, by sending fallen angels to earth to seduce and sleep with the daughters of men (**Genesis chapter 6**)... This did not work.

Next, when the devil realized that God had chosen a People through the Patriarchs (Abraham, Isaac, and Jacob) to fulfill His plan; the devil afflicted the wombs of these men' wives, in an attempt to prevent the birth of the Promised Seed.

Satan failed...

In due season, God always supernaturally opened the wombs of *the chosen women* and these women would conceive; birthing forth the ancestors of the **Chosen Seed.**

Throughout the history of God's chosen people, whenever Satan perceived that the birth of this special Seed was near, he would elevate evil men and send them out on a devilish mission to kill and destroy the newborn sons of Jewish women—in a futile-effort of destroying the **Child of Promise.**

But in spite of the devil's greatest efforts to abort the plan of God... the **Promised Seed** *would come.*

And HE did... For 33 years, the Son of God lived as a man. And for the last three and a half of those years, he walked the earth; healing the sick, raising the dead, casting out devils, opening blind eyes, and causing lame men to leap like harts... Finally, the Son of Man gave His life as a ransom for many. (**John 3:16**)

Jesus fulfills His mission and seals Satan's Fate

"And it was about the sixth hour (12p.m.), *and there was a darkness over all the earth until the ninth hour* (3p.m.). *And the sun was darkened, and the veil of the temple was rent in the midst. And when Jesus had cried with a loud voice, he said, Father, into thy hands I commend my spirit: and having said thus, he gave up the ghost."* (**Luke 23:44-46**)

The **Thief's** purpose for coming into the earth was *"for to steal and to kill and to destroy."* But God so loved the world that He sent His only Begotten Son into the world to suffer and die so that whosoever believeth in Him would not perish but have eternal life...

The **price** the Son of God would pay **for man's eternal redemption** would be His very own **life**.

Jesus prophesied in **John 3:14-15** and said: *"And as Moses lifted up the serpent in the wilderness even so must the Son of man be lifted up: That whosoever believeth in him should not perish, but have eternal life."*

And it came to pass...

Jesus was brutally beaten and nailed to a Roman cross. The cross was lifted up and dropped into a hole on the summit of Mt. Calvary, as the blood of the Son of God went gushing from his lacerated and pierced flesh, downwards; sprinkling the dusty earth with crimson drops.

Satan, unknowingly sealed his fate and lost his magnetic grip on man when he carried out his plan to crucify the Son of God... The god and princes of this world did not know...

Paul informed us in **I Corinthians, chapter 2 verse 8b** concerning the demonic blunder, "*...for had they known it, they would not have crucified the Lord of glory.*"

Jesus prophesied and said in **John 12:32**, "*And I, if I be lifted up from the earth, will draw all men unto me.*"

This was a mystery to Satan and his demons...

And they could not decipher it... They did not know. By crucifying our Lord and by *spilling the blood* of the Son of Man on the cross, the **Kingdom of Darkness** made a fatal and final mistake. Jesus outstretched hands on the cross, throughout the ages, would draw and beckon repentant men and women unto HIM.

In the **Old Covenant** or **Testament**, the blood of animals had to suffice for man's *atonement and cleansing* from the curse of the law of sin and death. But now, a better sacrifice had been enacted: Now, the blood of the only Begotten Son of God would serve as a sweet smelling savor before the nostrils of God, eternally canceling the enmity and wrath between a Holy God for every human creature who would, by grace through faith, accept Christ's precious sacrifice.

"But Christ being come an high priest of good things to come, by a greater and more perfect tabernacle, not made with hands, that is to say, not of this building; Neither by the blood of goats and calves, but by his own blood he entered in once into the holy place, having obtained eternal redemption for us." (**Hebrews 9:11-12**)

"And for this cause, he is the mediator of the New Testament, that by means of death, for the redemption of the transgressions that were under the first testament, they which are called might receive the promise of eternal inheritance." (**Hebrews 10:15**)

After Jesus died on the cross, entered Hades and rose from the dead with the Keys of Death and Hell, He proclaimed, *"I am he that liveth, and was dead; and, behold, I am alive for evermore, Amen; and have the keys of hell and of death."* (**Revelation 1:18**)

"And having spoiled principalities and powers, he made a shew of them openly, triumphing over them in it." (**Colossians 2:15**)

During the time that Paul wrote his letter to the Colossians church, Rome had the greatest army on the face of the earth... and the Roman Empire was consistently engaging in warfare, defeating other nations and tribes, in its ongoing pursuit to increase the Roman Treasury and territory.

When Rome would conquer a new nation or tribe, the Roman General who had gained the victory, would bring the king or tribal leader of that vanquished nation back to the city of Rome, along with his goods and possessions. And the general would parade the defeated leader—bound and naked through the streets of Rome. In other words, the Roman General would make an open show of the defeated leader; mocking and embarrassing him, as the conquered leader nakedly strode down the street before the spectating eyes of the Roman Senators and the citizens.

Jesus did likewise... Having defeated the devil and his crew, He took the keys of hell and death from Satan and he marched him and his demons, disgracefully, before His Father and the heavenly hosts... *"And having spoiled principalities and powers, he made a shew of them openly, triumphing over them in it."*

Afterward, Jesus spoke to his disciples: *"And he said unto them, Go ye into all the world, and preach the gospel to every creature. He that believeth and is baptized shall be save; but he that believeth not shall be damned. And these signs shall follow them that believe: In my name shall they cast out devils; they shall speak with new tongues; They shall take up serpents; and if they drink any deadly thing, it shall not hurt them; they shall lay hands on the sick, and they shall recover."* (**Mark 16:15-18**)

Not only did Christ give His eleven Apostles power over devils in the above text, but HE has also given every believer whom will believe in Him, the power to cast out devils—to be conquerors and to be ***triumphant*** over Satan and his satanic horde.

The Chief World Terrorist's last campaign

"But I would not have you to be ignorant, brethren, concerning them which are asleep, that ye sorrow not, even as others which have no hope. For if we believe that Jesus died and rose again, even so them also which sleep in Jesus will God bring with him. For this we say unto you by the word of the Lord, that we which are alive and remain unto the coming of the Lord shall not prevent them which are asleep. For the Lord himself shall descend from heaven with a shout, with the voice of the archangel, and with the trump of God: and the dead in Christ shall rise first: Then we which are alive and remain shall be caught up together with them in the clouds, to meet them in the air: and so shall we ever be with the Lord. Wherefore comfort one another with these words." (**I Thessalonians 4:13-18**)

But Before Satan launches his last campaign to destroy mankind and terrorize the earth; several things must occur:

First, Jesus Christ will appear in the clouds to rapture His church. God will rapture His church before He pours our His bitter cup or wrath upon the earth and release His flaming two-edged sword against the Anti-Christ whom will, after the rapture of the church, slowly make known his arrival upon the world scene.

"And as it was in the days of Noe, so shall it be also in the days of the Son of man. They did eat, they drank, they married wives, they were given in marriage, until the day that Noe entered into the ark, and the flood came, and destroyed them all. Likewise

also as it was in the days of Lot: they did eat, they drank, they bought, they sold, they planted, they builded; But the same day that Lot went out of Sodom it rained fire and brimstone from heaven, and destroyed them all. Even thus shall it be in the day when the Son of man is revealed." (**Luke 17:26-30**)

When the day of the coming of the Lord suddenly appears, the world will be going about its usual business; just as it was doing in the days of Noah and Lot. When Christ suddenly appears in the clouds to rapture His Church, people will be marrying and divorcing; eating and drinking; partying and shacking; and planting and building...

Debauchery will be at its worst.

Iniquity will greatly abound on planet earth because the liquified love of God in men' heart will have frozen and **waxed** cold.

Many who should be praying and watching will be asleep when our Lord and Savior Jesus Christ, as a thief in the night, suddenly appears. Like in the days of Noah and in the days of Lot, the unbeliever and the slothful will not be prepared.

Before God destroyed the world the first time, God told his servant Noah to build a boat and gather his family, along with two animals of every kind into the safety of the Ark.

When Noah and his family had safely entered the boat, God's vengeance fell—as clouds burst, flooding the earth with rain.

Water also shot up from the bowels of the deep; bombarding and submerging all the animals and people of the earth in murky-raging-waves of foaming-liquid-death.

Likewise... In the days of lot, God sent two angels to get Lot and his family and lead them out of the twin cities of Sodom and Gomorrah before in acting His vengeance... When Lot and his family were safely out of the city, God's judgment and wrath felled—raining and thundering upon Sodom and Gomorrah, fire and brimstone.

Paul tells us in the book of **I Thessalonians, chapter 4** that Believers should *"comfort one another"* with the good news that *we will not all sleep* (physically die).

The soul and spirit of Believers who have died before being **caught up** in the rapture, will instantly be with our Lord. *"To be absence from the body is to be present with the Lord"* is what the Bible teaches us.

Thus, the dead in Christ will return with HIM in the clouds when He comes to rapture His church.

I Corinthians 15:51-53 reads, *"Behold, I shew you a mystery; We shall not all sleep, but we shall all be changed. In a moment, in the twinkling of an eye, at the last trump: for the trumpet shall sound, and the dead shall be raised incorruptibly, and we shall be changed. For this corruptible must put on incorruption, and this mortal must put on immortality."*

In the above text, Paul unravels for us a mystery. He lets us know this: **as children of God, all of us will not physically die.**

"...we shall not all sleep...", Paul encourages us. But as quick as one can blink one's eye, the living saints will be caught up to meet Christ in the air when our Lord Jesus Christ suddenly appears.

When this occurs, the **spirits** and **souls** of the dead in Christ will already be with the Lord. Paul says: *"But I would not have you to be ignorant brethren, concerning them which are sleep that ye sorrow not, even as other which have no hope. For if we believe that Jesus died and rose again, even so them also which sleep in Jesus will God bring with hi*m." (**I Thessalonians 4:13-14**)

Let me more clearly explain the above text: When Christians die, their soul and spirit are ushered by angels into the third heaven to be immediately with the Lord. **The souls and spirits of all believers are at this very moment in heaven.** (Read my book, **"By My Spirit"**, for more detailed information on this Biblical fact).

When Christ comes to rapture His church, the Believers who are alive on the earth will in a moment, in the twinkling of an eye, be physically changed as their corruptible bodies put on incorruption and their **whole being** (*body, soul* and *spirit*) are caught up in the clouds to meet the Lord Jesus Christ in the air.

Since the dead-in-Christ souls and spirits are already with Christ; *their bodies or physical remains*, whether it be the **whole cadaver**; or only **bones**, **ashes** or **dust**—at the sound of the trumpet they will be instantly changed...

The **physical bodies** of the dead in Christ will be caught up into the clouds to be with our Lord in the air.

The **bodies** of *the dead-in-Christ shall rise first.*

"...the dead in Christ shall rise first..."

Therefore, when the **bodies, souls** and **spirits** of the living saints are caught up to meet the Lord in the air, the **bodies, souls** and **spirit** of the **physically deceased-in-the-Lord** will be already there.... waiting in the air.

The same Spirit that raised Christ from the dead shall quicken our mortal bodies and raise us up.

After the Church is taken from the earth, the devil, having less restraint, will make his move. Cloaked in anonymity, the **Anti-Christ** will quietly, throughout the next three and a half years, ease his way upon the world scene. And in the last 3 and half years of the Great Tribulation, the **Anti-Christ** will thoroughly and radically reveal himself.

The Anti-Christ (1st Beast) Charismatic World Leader: *"And I stood upon the sea, and saw a beast rise up out of the sea, having seven heads and ten horns, and upon his horns ten crowns, and upon his heads the name of blasphemy. And the beast which I saw was like unto a leopard, and his feet were as the feet of a bear, and his mouth as the mouth of a lion: and the dragon gave him his power, and his seat, and great authority. And I saw one of his heads as it were wounded to death; and his deadly wound was healed: and all the world wondered after the beast. And they worshiped the dragon which gave power unto the beast: and they worshiped the beast, saying, "Who is like unto the beast? Who is able to make war with him?" And there was given unto him a mouth speaking great things and blasphemies; and power was given unto him to continue forty and two months. And he opened his mouth in blasphemy against God, to blaspheme his name, and his tabernacle, and them that* *dwell in heaven. And it was given unto him to make war with the saints, and to overcome them: and power was given him over all kindreds, and tongues, and nations. And all that dwell upon the earth shall worship him, whose names are not written in the book of life of the Lamb slain from the foundation of the world."* **(Revelation 13:1-8)**

After the rapture of the Church (the literal disappearance of millions off the face of the earth) the world will be in chaos. Fear, famine, pestilence, earthly disasters and wars will join hands to choke and squeeze humanity into a desperate search for relief.

And then the Anti-Christ will appear with answers, offering solutions to the world's problems. His only request in return will be that the world leaders accept him as **the supreme ruler** of the planet earth and denounce the God of heaven and worship him and him alone.

He'll offer the world: **life**, **peace**, **physical health** and **prosperity**. But behind these false promises, right on the heels, will be *sudden destruction... and death.*

The Dragon (2nd Beast), Devil: *"And I beheld another beast coming up out of the earth; and he had two horns like a lamb, and he spake as a dragon. And he exerciseth all the power of the first beast before him, and causeth the earth and them which dwell therein to worship the first beast, whose deadly wound was healed. And he doeth great wonders, so that he maketh fire come down from heaven on the earth in the sight of men, And deceiveth them that dwell on the earth by the means of those miracles which he had power to do in the sight of the beast;*

saying to them that fell on the earth, that they should make an image to the beast which had the wound by the sword, and did live." **(Revelation 13:11-14)**

The Dragon or Devil will be the power source behind the Anti-Christ. The Dragon will cause *"the earth and them which dwell therein to worship the first beast..."* through the demonstration of supernatural acts and the workings of signs and wonders. He will also make the people of the earth chose the **image of the beast** (the false prophet) as the representative and spokesperson for the **Anti-Christ.**

The False Prophet (Beast's Image): *"And he* (the dragon) *had power to give life unto the image of the beast, that the image of the beast should both speak, and cause that as many as would not worship the image of the beast should be killed. And he causeth all, both small and great, rich and poor, free and bond, to receive a mark in their right hand, or in their foreheads: and that no man might buy or sell, save he that had the mark, or the name of the beast, or the number of his name."* **(Revelation 13:15-17)**

The Anti-Christ will appear upon the world scene after the rapture of the church of God, but he will not come alone. He will bring help...

God is a **Triune Being: Father, Son** and **Holy Ghost.**

Thus, to imitate the Holy Trinity, the devil will come in the triune-form of **Anti-Christ, Dragon** and **False Prophet**—in his campaign to deceive and terrorize an already confused and tormented world.

Revelation 16: 13,14 and **16** reads, *"And I saw three unclean spirits like frogs come out of the mouth of the dragon, and out of the mouth of the beast, and out of the mouth of the false prophet. For they are the spirits of devils, working miracles, which go forth unto the kings of the earth and of the whole world, to gather them to the battle of that great day of God Almighty... And he gathered them together into a place called in the Hebrew tongue Armageddon."*

In the text above, the **Dragon**, **Anti-Christ** and **False Prophet** prepare for battle in the earth, by gathering a diabolic military horde of men, demons and fallen angels.

From the Third Heaven, our Lord and Savior Jesus Christ is also descending upon the earth with HIS army for the impending battle.

*"And I saw heaven opened and behold a white horse; and he that sat upon him was called **Faithful and True**, and in righteousness he doth judge and make war. His eyes were as a flame of fire, and on his head were many crowns; and he had a name written, that no man knew, but he himself. And he was clothed with a vesture dipped in blood: and his name is called the Word of God. And the armies which were in heaven followed him upon white horses, clothed in fine linen, white and clean. And out of his mouth goeth a sharp sword, that with it he should smite the nations: and he shall rule them with a rod of iron: and he threadeth the winepress of the fierceness and wrath of Almighty God. And he hath on his vesture and on his thigh a name written, King of Kings and Lord of Lords."* (**Revelation 19:11-16**)

The Battle

"And I saw the beast, and the kings of the earth, and their armies, gathered together to make war against him that sat on the horse, and against his army. And the beast was taken, and with him the false prophet that wrought miracles before him, with which he deceived them that received the mark of the beast, and them that worshiped his image. These both were cast alive into a lake of fire burning with brimstone. And the remnant were slain with the sword of him that sat upon the horse, which sword proceeded out of his mouth: and all the fowls were filled with their flesh." (**Revelation 19:19-21**)

The battle of Armageddon ends with the multitudes of sinners and rebellious nations being slain by the sword (Word) which proceeded from the mouth of the **Warrior and King on the white horse.** And the **False Prophet** and **Antichrist**, whom had *triode* with the devil to gather the wicked army are now defeated. And they are both are immediately cast into the **Lake of Fire...** *for all eternity.*

The Dragon is Bound

"And I saw an angel come down from heaven, having the key of the bottomless pit and a great chain in his hand. And he laid hold on the dragon, that old serpent, which is the Devil, and Satan, and bound him a thousand years, And cast him into the bottomless pit; and shut him up, and set a seal upon him, that he should deceive the nations no more, till the thousand years should

be fulfilled: and after that he must be loosed a little season." **(Revelation 20:1-3)**

After Jesus and His army triumphs in the battle of Armageddon, Jesus sets up His reign in the city of Jerusalem for a thousand years. Meanwhile, the Devil is bound in a bottomless pit. He's now incarcerated, angry and agitated and seething for another opportunity to deceive the nations.

Meanwhile, the immortal martyred tribulation saints, the saved tribulation surviving saints; along with the returned raptured saints are in Jerusalem, in the presence of the **Lord Jesus Christ**... at peace...reigning triumphantly with Him for a thousand years.

"...And I saw the souls of them that were beheaded for the witness of Jesus, and for the word of God, and which had not worshipped the beast, neither his image, neither had received his mark upon their foreheads, or in their hands; and they lived and reigned with Christ a thousand years." **(Revelation 20:4)**

During the Tribulation period and after the culmination of this seven years epic with the battle of Armageddon, there will be men, women, boys and girls in the earth who will accept Jesus Christ as their Lord and Savior and who by God's grace survive this horrific season.

There will also be babies who will be born during the Tribulation period who will survive into the Millennial Reign of Christ.

I believe some adult sinners will also, by the mercy and grace of God, survive the tribulation period and enter into the Millennial reign of Christ.

Therefore, there will be both sinners and saints upon the earth, alive in the flesh, when Christ began His thousand year reign. Unfortunately, some of the sinners who will be alive during Jesus Millennial reign will *refuse to* receive HIM as **Lord and Savior**... They will not be saved.

During this millennial reign, many of the sinners and saints who are still in their Adamic bodies will procreate and produce children. And some of these Millennial born children will grow up and will also refuse to accept Christ as their Lord and Savior.........

They too will be forever lost.

For 1000 years, Christ will sat on the throne of David in the city of Jerusalem and rule His people (some will be in their **mortal bodies** and others in their **immortal bodies**).

With righteousness, love, joy and peace, the Lord will reign. After this 1000 years is over, Satan will be loosed once again to corrupt and deceive those sinners in the earth who would not accept Christ as their Lord and Savior during HIS Millennial reign.

Satan's Final Bow
(The Curtain Closes)

"And when the thousand years are expired, Satan shall be loosed out of his prison, and shall go out to deceive the nations which are in the four quarters of the earth, Gog and Magog, to gather them together to battle: the number of whom is as the sand of the sea. And they went up on the breadth of the earth,

and compassed the camp of the saints about, and the beloved city: and fire came down from God out of heaven, and devoured them. And the devil that deceived them was cast into the lake of fire and brimstone, where the beast and the false prophet are, and shall be tormented day and night for ever and ever." **(Revelation 20:7-10)**

After the **Millennium** there will be the final battle between good and evil; the devil will be permanently defeated and in a larva lake of fire and brimstone, he will meet his final fate.

For **Eternity** he will reside there, in perpetual captivity, for his treasonous acts against God and for his evil works perpetrated against mankind and against the demons and angels whom he corrupted and beguiled into following him.

"And I saw a great white throne, and him that sat on it, from whose face the earth and the heaven fled away; and there was found no place for them. And I saw the dead, small and great, stand before God: and the books were opened: and another book was opened, which is the book of life; and the dead were judged out of those things which were written in the books, according to their works. And the sea gave up the dead which were in it; and death and hell delivered up the dead which were in them: and they were judged every man according to their works. And death and hell were cast into the lake of fire. This is the second death. And whosoever was not found written in the book of life was cast into the lake of fire." **(Revelation 20:11-15)**

In this **Lake of Fire,** along with the Dragon (devil), the Anti-Christ and the False Prophet will be there, with fallen angels and demons, and the souls of all the humans throughout the Earth's Adamic age, who would not accept the **Lord Jesus Christ**, as their **God and Savior**. They will be screaming, gnawing and gnashing their teeth—bitterly crying out for mercy in this eternal fiery place of gross-darkness and torment.

If you have read this book and you're not saved, I would like to give you good news... You don't have to go to this dreadful place which was created for the devil and his angels... There's room at the cross for you!

Romans 10:9-10 assured us with these words: "... *if thou shalt confess with thy mouth the Lord Jesus, and shalt believe in thine heart that God hath raised him from the dead, thou shalt be saved. For with the heart man believeth unto righteousness; and with the mouth confession is made unto salvation.*"

John 3:16-17 states, "*For God so loved the world, that he gave his only begotten Son that whosoever believeth in him should not perish, but have everlasting life. For God sent not his Son into the world to condemn the world; but that the world through him might be saved.*"

Let's Pray: Lord, I have once again written what you have given me to give to the people. You did not give me this book for men to live in fear of the devil but you gave me this book so that those who read it might know that you're God and surrender to your **Lordship** by accepting Your Son **Christ Jesus** as Lord and Savior; and after having receive Christ into their hearts and lives, they may personally and forever know the reality of these scriptures: "*Greater is He that* *is in me than he that is in the world."* And *"If God be for us, who can be against us."*

Lord, I pray that you **touch, bless** and **save** all who read this book, and that you will show them, by **Your Spirit**; how precious they are in Your sight.

Knowing that you have answered this prayer Lord Jesus, I, now by faith, give you *praise and glory* which is always due Your Name. *Glory.......Glory Be to God! Praise be to God in the highest and to Him be all the Glory!!!*

In Jesus Name. **Hallelujah!!!**

EPILOGUE

The bulk of the material in this book, **Exposing The Devil,** was written and designed to give the reader a complete biographical sketch of the entire life of **Lucifer/Satan.** This book was written to give a portrait of the devil's rise and fall and to also inform the reader of some of his geographical dwelling places and his various jobs and his selfish-agenda. This book has informed you of *his many names*, *his twisted nature* and *his evil character...* and finally this book has exhibited the devil in his ultimate abode, the **Lake of Fire—** the final dwelling place where Our Almighty God has judged and sentenced him to forever.

In the beginning of this book, we first saw Lucifer in his pomp and glory but as time and the pages of this book turned, we eventually saw Lucifer become the devil and we gradually saw his doomed-and-tragic ending in the Eternal Lake of Fire.

Since I have given the readers of this book such a vivid and shocking view of the devil and his plight to the Lake of Fire, I feel that it would be remiss of me if I did not give my readers a glimpse of the New Heaven and Earth that our Lord Jesus Christ returned to His Kingdom to prepare for us (those who love Him).

Whereas the devil and humans who will not repent and accept Christ have no hope, the people who accept Christ have an *assured, eternal* and *blessed-hope.*

In **John, chapter fourteen**, **verses one through three**, Jesus consoles His disciples with these words, when He informs them of His soon earthly departure: *"Let not your heart be troubled: ye believe in God, believe also in me. In my Father's house are many **mansions**: if it were not so, I would have told you. I go to prepare a place for you. And if I go and prepare a place for you; I will come again, and receive you unto myself; that where I am, there ye may be also."*

The word for **mansion** in the Greek is **mone** (pronounced **mon-ay**). This term refers to a residence, abode or dwelling place. The word mansion in our English language means: *a large stately home or a very big house with many rooms.*

One of the reasons Jesus told his disciple that he must go back to the Third Heaven is because He, as the Master Carpenter and Chief Architect had a building project He had to attend to: *"I go and prepare a place for you."*

For about 2000 years now, Jesus, our Messiah, has been working on a resident for us in Heaven. He has been preparing a glorious and splendid place to receive His **Beloved Church** and **Bride**.

In the beginning, it took our Lord six days to complete the heaven and earth, but He has now spent about 2000 years working on a dwelling place for us. He's being very meticulous and methodical... every detail must be *just right* for His **Beloved**.

His heart's longing and desire is this: *"Father, I will that they also, whom thou hast given me, be with me where I am, that*

71

they may behold my glory, which thou hast given me, for thou lovedst me before the foundation of the world." (**John 17:24**)

Jesus' heart pants and yearns for us to be with Him in His heavenly home so that we may behold His Eternal Splendor and Glory... but we must be patient and wait. *"For yet a little while, and He that shall come will come, and will not tarry."* (**Hebrews 10:37**)

However, several things must happen before the new Heaven and Earth our Lord is preparing for us will be presented for our habitation. First the rapture must occur (this is when Christ returns in the air, adorned in shekenah clouds of glory to catch up his Church).

"For the Lord himself shall descend from heaven with a shout; with the voice of the archangel, and with the trump of God: and the dead in Christ shall rise first: 'Then we which are alive and remain shall be caught up together with them in the clouds, to meet the Lord in the air: and so shall we ever be with the Lord." (**I Thessalonians 4:16,17**)

"Behold, I shew you a mystery; We shall not all sleep, but we shall all be changed. In a moment, in the twinkling of an eye, at the last trump: for the trumpet shall sound, and the dead shall be raised incorruptible, and we shall be changed. For this corruptible must put on incorruption, and this mortal must put on immortality." (**I Corinthians 15:51-53**)

After the ***rapture*** or the ***catching away*** of the Church, the Anti-Christ, False Prophet and Dragon (devil), now having no restraint from the saints of God, will appear on the

World's scene. There will then be seven years of tribulation such as the world has never know.

For seven years, this Demonic-Trio will cause mass chaos and wreck world-wide havoc as God, during this same period, pours His bitter cup of wrath out upon the earth.

During the last three and half-years of the seven year period, the tribulation will intensify as God loose reign for this Demonic-Trio to do their worst. (**What a horrible time! What great Tribulation!** {Read Revelation 13-18})

The Tribulation period will end with a battle between Good and Evil, referred to by theologians as the **Battle of Armageddon**.

The Lion of the Tribe of Judah (Jesus) easily wins the Battle. And two third of this demonic-trio—the **Anti-Christ** and **False Prophet** will be cast into the **Lake of Fire**, forever, to never rise again (read **Revelation, chapter 19**). After these two characters are dealt with, Christ will order one of his angels to bind Satan; that old serpent the devil, and cast him into a bottomless pit and seal it for 1000 years. (read **Revelation 20:1-3**)

During this 1000 years, while Satan is incarcerated in the bottomless pit, our Lord Jesus Christ will reign in Jerusalem, seated on the throne of David. This period is referred to by theologians as **Christ's Millennial Reign.**

After the thousand years are up, Satan will be loosed for a season to once again deceive the nations. He will gather up an army composed of demons, fallen angels and men and they will surround Jerusalem in a futile attempt to conquer

Christ seat of power and glory, but God will rain down fire upon Satan and his cohorts from heaven and instantly defeat them. (**Revelation 20:9**)

Satan is then cast into the **Lake of Fire...** His **Kingdom of Darkness** immediately comes to a sad and everlasting end. (see **Revelation 20:10**)

Now, it is time for Christ to present the New Heaven and Earth which he has for so long been preparing for his **Beloved Church** and **Bride.**

"And I saw a new heaven and a new earth: for the first heaven and the first earth were passed away: and there was no more sea. And I John saw the holy city, New Jerusalem coming down from God out of heaven, prepared as a bride adorned for her husband. And I heard a great voice out of heaven saying, Behold, the tabernacle of God is with men, and he will dwell with them and they shall be his people, and God himself shall be with them, and be their God. And God shall wipe away all tears from their eyes: and there shall be no more death, neither sorrow, nor crying, neither shall there be any more pain: for the former things are passed away." (**Revelation 21:1-4**)

"And there came unto me one of the seven angels which had the seven vials full of the seven last plagues, and talked with me, saying, Come hither, I will shew thee the bride, the Lamb's wife. And he carried me away in the spirit to a great and high mountain, and shewed me that great city, the holy Jerusalem, descending out of heaven from God, having the glory of God: and her light was like unto a stone most precious, even like a jasper stone, clear as crystal: And had a wall great and high, and had twelve gates and

at the gates twelve angels, and names written thereon which are the names of the twelve tribes of the children of Israel. On the east three gates; on the north three gates; on the south three gates, and on the west three gates. And the wall of the city had twelve foundations, and on them the names of the twelve apostles of the Lamb...And the building of the wall of it was of jasper; and the city was pure gold, like unto clear glass. And the foundation of the wall of the city were garnished with all manner of precious stones. The first foundation was jasper; the second sapphire; the third, a chalcedony; the fourth, an emerald; the fifth sardonyx; the sixth, sardius; the seventh, chrysolite, the eight, beryl; the ninth, a topaz; the tenth, a chrysoprasus; the eleventh, a jacinth; the twelfth, an amethyst. And the twelve gates were twelve pearls; every several gate was of one pearl: and the street of the city was pure gold, as it were transparent glass. And I saw a temple therein: for the Lord God Almighty and the Lamb are the temple of it. And the city had no need of the sun neither of the moon to shine in it: for the glory of God did lighten it, and the Lamb is the light thereof."(**Revelation 21:9-14, 18-23**)

"And he shewed me a pure river of water of life, clear as crystal, proceeding out of the throne of God and of the Lamb. In the midst of the street of it, and on either side of the river, was there the tree of life, which bare twelve manner of fruits, and yielded her fruit every month: and the leaves of the tree were for the healing of the nations. And there shall be no more curse: but the throne of God and of the Lamb shall be in it; and his servants shall serve him: And they shall see his face: and his name shall be in their foreheads. And there shall be no night there; and they

need no candle, neither light of the sun: for the Lord God giveth them light: and they shall reign for ever and ever." (**Revelation 22:1-5**)

My brothers and sisters, our **Lord** and **Kinsman Redeemer** is preparing for us a new heaven and earth—and a glorious city called New Jerusalem for us to dwell in with him throughout all eternity. We will one day cast aside these corruptible bodies and put on incorruptible ones; *immortal and glorious bodies* that are able to travel through tangible objects and space and explore the *endless beauties* of worlds without end. Everywhere we go in our new bodies and every place we visit, out Lord will be with us...for in **Him** (that **Brilliant LIGHT**), we'll live and move and have our being.

Forever and ever, we'll be able to worship and thank our Lord for loving us and saving us, as we admire the stripes on His back, the wound in His side and the nail prints in His hands and feet. Throughout an endless eternity, we'll praise and worship our Savior as we endeavor to comprehend how much our **LORD** love us for Him to have suffered and died and shed His **BLOOD** on a rugged wooden cross in order to redeem us...... *and so richly lavish us with life in His Everlasting Luminous Presence.*

Hosanna! Hosanna! Hosanna!
HALLELUJAH!!!
Let everything that has breath
praise the Lord!!!

APPENDIX

EXPOSING MAN'S SOUL

(...*ANOTHER POTENTIALLY POWERFUL AND DEADLY ENEMY*)

In the nineteen seventies, there was a variety comedy show with a flamboyant and talented young black man, named Flip Wilson that came on every week. Flip Wilson was loved and was watched by not only black folks but the white audience loved him as well. Flip Wilson made a certain saying of his very popular. When he would do something outrageous or sinister he would stare into the camera and say with a slight smile upon his face: "*The devil made me do it.*"

In this book, I have exposed the devil, but now I must expose another potentially deadly enemy of man... it is *man's own soul*. I know many of my readers have heard the saying that our enemy is: **the world, the flesh** and **the devil**. This saying is true but I would like to rephrase it a little and say that our enemy is: **the world, the soul-controlled-flesh** and **the devil**.

First let me explain how the world is man's potential enemy. **Satan** is the **prince** or **god** of this world and he sets and controls through people, things, and circumstances, the tempo of this worldly cosmos.

He influences the souls of men and women through fashions, movies, television, radio programs, magazines, books...and through people influencing other people. If the devil can insert one bad apple —that rotten fruit has the potential to destroy the whole basket. That is why Paul warns us, *"...be not conformed to this world but to be transformed by the renewing of your mind."*

The Apostle John tells us to love not the world but instead our love must be focused on God and toward our fellowman. We, as children of God, are in the world but we are not of the world.

I have spent the first three chapters of this book informing you that the devil is the archenemy of man's soul—so it would be redundant to elaborate on that perspective again.

What I will inform and warn you of now is how the soul of a saint (a born-again believer) can be his or her worst enemy—if that soul is not **disciplined by the Word of God** and if it is not *subservient to the Believer's born-again spirit and the Spirit of God.*

What is the soul?

Before I answer this question, I must first tell you who man is. Like his Creator (God), man is a **triune-being**, composed of **body, soul** and **spirit. I Thessalonians 5:23** reads, *"And the very God of peace sanctify you wholly: and I pray God your whole spirit and soul and body be preserved blameless unto the coming of our Lord Jesus Christ."*

Let's read **Genesis 2:27**: *"And the Lord God formed man of the dust of the ground* (carbon elements which make up the **human body**) *and breathed into his nostrils the breath of life* (**spirit**); *and man became a **living soul**."*

In the Hebrew, the word for spirit is **Ruach**, and in the Greek, the word for spirit is **Pneuma**. These words translated into English means, **wind, air, breath...**"

In these verses, I have extracted from **Genesis** and **I Thessalonians**, we clearly see the *tri-unity* of man: **body, soul** and **spirit**. Some charismatic word preachers have read **Genesis 2:27** and came to the fraudulent conclusion that man is a **spirit**...that **his basic essence is spirit**. Their argument is: that if God breathed from **His Spirit** into the dust he fashioned in His Own Image to produce life, that man too must be a **spirit**...and if God breathed **His Spirit** into man that man must also be **god** because of **God's Breath or Spirit** that resides within him.

These preachers have good intentions, but this argument that man's basic makeup is **spirit** and that he is a **god** can be dangerous and detrimental to the body of Christ.

The late Gilbert Earl Patterson, the former presiding Bishop of the Church of God in Christ, being a charismatic-word preacher himself, did not go along with this doctrine. Bishop is at rest now, in the presence of our Lord and Savior, but his message was not lost. I will proclaim that man became a living soul like Scripture teaches us, along-side others who believe that man **basic essence** is **soul**, until the Lord call me home to be with Him.

Sincere men and women of God have been led astray by this false belief that the **basic essence** of man is **spirit**. I pray that the Holy Scriptures and the Holy Spirit that is within believers enlighten them to this truth: Man is not a **spirit** who has a **soul** and lives in a **body** but man is a **soul** who has a **spirit** and lives in a **body**. The basic essence of man is **soul**.

Solomon said in **Ecclesiastes 12:6-7**, "*Or ever the silver cord be loosed, or the golden bowl be broken or the pitcher be broken at the fountain, or the wheel broken at the cistern. Then shall the dust return to the earth as it was: and the spirit shall return unto God who gave it.*"

Solomon teaches that the **spirit** or **Breath of God** is only loaned unto men. After a man's body is worn out or has sprung a leak (when a man dies), the spirit leaves it and returns to God who gave it. "*The body without the spirit is dead.*"

Know this fact: When a man dies who has accepted Christ precious blood as atonement for his sin, that man's spirit and soul as one entity returns to God. Eventually, when his body is raised incorruptibly from the dead, the man will forever joyfully exist in the Creator's presence as a triune being—**body**, **soul** and **spirit**.

If a man does not accept Christ as his Lord and Savior and he die without repenting; that man's **spirit** (*life giving force*) will return to God who gave it and that man's **soul**, separated from the **Life** and **Spirit of God**, will find itself in hell awaiting his body which on the day of judgment will also be cast into the lake of fire.

The bible doesn't say that the **spirit** that sinneth shall surely die. But it does warn us that the **soul** that sinneth shall sure die.

Matthew 10:28 reads, *"And fear not them which kill the body, but are not able to kill the soul; but fear him which is able to destroy both soul and body in hell."*

Jesus himself said in **Mark 8:36-37,** *"For what shall it profit a man, if he shall gain the whole world, and lose his own soul? Or what shall a man give in exchange for his soul?"*

Man is a soul.

If man's basic makeup was **spirit**, I would not have to write an addendum to this book. If man was fundamentally a **spirit-being,** the moment a man accepts Christ Jesus as Lord and Savior and **God's Spirit** comes and abide in his **spirit**, that man's spirit would then be perfectly lead by the **Spirit of God** and he would not have to overcome the obstacles of the **soul** (his **mind**, will and **emotions**).

But since man is a **living soul**—and the devil knows this—man must first conquer and break through the soulical realm before he can walk in his **born-again spirit man** which God made new the very moment he believed and invited Christ into his life and **God's Spirit** entered him.

Paul tells us in **Philippians 2:12-13**, *"Wherefore, my beloved, as ye have always obeyed, not as in my presence only, but now much more in my absence, work out your own salvation with fear and trembling. For it is God which worketh in you both to will and to do of his good pleasure."*

As I mentioned at the beginning of this chapter, Flip Wilson made this saying very popular in the 70's, "*The devil made me do it.*"

Let me clear up some erroneous things and give you some facts: **We blame too much on the devil**.

If you're a believer, the devil does not and he cannot make you do anything. But he does contrive and manipulate people, circumstances and problems to vex and test the **souls** (minds, wills, and emotions) of saved men and women.

Satan does this, because he know that the only way a believer can please and serve God is when his **mind**, **will** and **emotions** are yielded completely to his **born-again spirit man** and to the **Spirit of God**.

When the devil came to tempt Jesus after Jesus had fasted for forty days and night in the **fourth chapters** of the gospels of **Matthew** and **Luke**, the devil could not tempt our Lord—he failed. The reason the devil could not tempt Christ was not because Jesus was God; although He was...

Remember, Jesus was also a hundred percent man and as a man, he was physically tired and hungry. The reason the devil could not tempt Christ is because, our Lord was walking in the **Spirit** and his **human spirit** *was totally yielded* to **the Spirit of His Father in heaven;** therefore the devil found nothing in Christ to tempt... It was not so with Peter.

"And the Lord said, Simon, Simon, behold, Satan hath desired to have you, that he may sift you as wheat: But I have prayed for thee, that thy faith fail not: and when thou art converted, strengthen thy brethren." (**Luke 22:21-32**)

What did Jesus mean when he told his disciple Simon Peter, that the devil wanted to sift him. "...*Satan hath desired to have you that he may sift you as wheat.*"

What did Satan want to do to Peter... What does, "*sift you as wheat mean*"?

As we examine the gospels, we'll discover exactly what: *sifting Peter as wheat meant...* And in the following verses, we'll see some of the things Satan did to Simon Peter, and influenced Simon Peter to do.

Immediately, after Jesus warned Peter of the devil's plan, Peter retorted in **verse 33** of **Luke 22**: "*And he* (Peter) *said, I am ready to go with thee, both into prison, and to death.*" Peter meant this: He was willing to go to prison with his master or even die with him.

Now this is where the sifting comes in. The devil had put Peter under his microfying glass and observed Peter thoroughly... He observed Peter while he was awake and even in his sleep. "*Where is Peter's weakness*", Satan pondered, as he sifted through Peter's background, family history and his psyche (psychological makeup)? The devil found something in Peter... It was insecurity and fear.

Jesus spoke: "*And he said, I tell thee, Peter, the cock shall not crow this day, before that thou shalt thrice deny that thou knowest me.*"

And just as Jesus said it, it happened. Peter denied that he even knew Jesus and he did it **3** times before a rooster crowed.

In **Matthew chapter 16**, we read this story: *"From that time forth began Jesus to show unto his disciples, how that he must go unto Jerusalem, and suffer many things of the elders and chief priests and scribes, and be killed, and be raised again the third day. Then Peter took him, and began to rebuke him, saying, Be it far from thee, Lord: this shall not be unto thee. But he turned, and said unto* the devil who was using Peter, *"Get thee behind me, Satan: thou art an offense unto me: for thou savourest not the things that be of God, but those that be of men."* (**Matthew 16:21-23**)

When Jesus tried to inform his disciples of his destiny, Peter didn't want to hear it... Jesus came into the world to die for mankind. John quoted it best. *"For God so loved the world that he gave his only begotten Son that whosoever believeth in him should not perish but have everlasting life."* (**John 3:16**)

In **Matthew chapter 16**, the devil found a flaw in Peter... This time, it was Peter's selfish love and Peter's egotistic desire to keep Christ by his side.

Instead of Peter savoring or relishing the things of God, Peter wanted his own desire fulfilled. He wanted perpetual fellowship with Christ on earth. But **Christ's** sole purpose was to die... to do the work the Father had sent him to do.

Roman 12, verses one and **two** read, *"I Beseech you therefore, brethren, by the mercies of God, that ye present your bodies a living sacrifice, holy, acceptable unto God, which is your reasonable service. And be not conformed to this world: but be ye transformed by the renewing of your mind that ye may prove what is that good, and acceptable, and perfect will of God."*

The soul consists of the **mind, will** and **emotions**.

Thus, the believer *must renew* **his mind, will** *and emotions* through the word of God by allowing his **born-again spirit man** and the **Holy Spirit** within him to lead and guide him into all Truth. Paul said in **Romans chapter 8**, that if a believer would *walk in the Spirit*, he would not fulfill the lust of the flesh.

If Satan can, *through chaos and the power of suggestion*, keep us from renewing our minds with the Word of God and from reigning-in and controlling our emotions and will with God's Word, he can keep us defeated, even when we're fill with the Spirit.

I will once again, in an effort to validate my argument for the **soul** being a potential enemy, repeat *an established fact*: A **man's soul** consists of his **mind**, his **will** and his **emotions**.

The Apostle Paul, unlike most preachers today, gives an honest testimony of struggles he experienced with his flesh and how, through the Spirit of God, he overcame them. Let's go to **Romans chapter seven.**

"But sin, taking occasion by the commandment, wrought in me all manner of concupiscence. For without the law sin was dead. For I was alive without the law once: but when the commandment came, sin revived, and I died. And the commandment, which was ordained to life, I found to be unto death. For sin, taking occasion by the commandment, deceived me, and by it slew me." (**Romans 7:8-11**)

"For we know that the law is spiritual: but I am carnal sold under sin. For that which I do I allow not: for what I would,

85

that do I not; but what I hate, that do I. If then I do that which I would not, I consent unto the law that it is good. Now then it is no more I that do it, but sin that dwelleth in me (that is, in my flesh), dwelleth no good thing: for to will is present with me; but how to perform that which is good I find not. For the good that I would do I do not: but the evil which I would not, that I do... I find then a law, that, when I would do good, evil is present with me. For I delight in the law of God after the inward man: But I wee another law in my members, waring against the law of my mind, and bringing me into captivity to the law of sin which is in my members. O Wretched man that I am! Who shall deliver me from the body of this death? I thank God through Jesus Christ our Lord. So then with the mind I myself serve the law of God; but with the flesh the law of sin." (**Romans 7:14-19, 21-25**)

In **Romans chapter seven,** the Apostle Paul had a **will** problem. He wanted to obey God's laws and do what was right but he kept finding himself giving in to the flesh. Paul states, "*For I know that in me (that is, in my flesh) dwelleth no good thing: for to **will** is present with me; but how to perform that which is good, I find not.*"

Paul wanted to do what was right but he did not know how to shift his **will** into forward gear... He was stuck in neutral... in a cycle of spiritual defeat.

Finally Paul cried out, "*O wretched man that I am! Who shall deliver me from the body of this death?*"

Our Lord Jesus Christ then reveals to Paul his dilemma, "*So then with the mind I myself serve the law of God; but with the flesh the law of sin.*"

Paul's problem was this: With the mind, (I **MYSELF**.)

Paul was trying to live a victorious Christian life through his own **mind** and **will**... he was operating in the soulical realm.

But then, Christ gives Paul the solution: "*There is therefore now no condemnation to them which are in Christ Jesus, who walk not after the flesh, but after the Spirit.*"

The solution for Paul and for every Christian who will live victorious is to submit their **body** (flesh) and **soul** (mind, will and emotions) to their born-again **spirit** man and *walk after the* **Spirit**.

"*For what the law could not do, in that it was weak through the flesh, God sending his own Son in the likeness of sinful flesh, and for sin, condemned sin in the flesh: That the righteousness of the law might be fulfilled in us **who walk not after the flesh, but after the Spirit.**"* (**Roman 8: 3-4**)

If we are to be victorious Christians, we must learn how to allow the **Word of God** to control our **mind**, **will** and **emotions**. Paul said, "*For though we walk in the flesh, we do not war after the flesh: (For the weapons of our warfare are not carnal, but mighty through God to the pulling down of strong holds;) casting down imaginations, and every high thing that exalteth itself against the knowledge of God, and bringing into captivity every thought to the obedience of Christ.*" (**II Corinthians 10:3-5**)

When the world, the flesh or the devil brings negative thoughts to our mind, we must through the Spirit and Word of God cast them down. We must learn to bring our **body** and

soul under the subjection of our **born-again spirit man**—in compliance and obedience to God's Spirit; by allowing God's Word to dwell richly in us.

We must also learn how to manage our emotions so that we're not be so easily intimidated, upset or shaken.

If you are a Born-again Believer and the doctor tell you today that you have cancer and that you have less than six months to live; you cannot and must not allow the *demonic spirit of fear* to rule your **mind**, **will** and **emotions** and cause you to lose hope. Cast down those negative thoughts and grab hold to the **Word** and proclaim, *"I will live and not die and do the works of the Lord."* And ask yourself this question: *"Is there anything too hard for God?"*

We, as Saints, must not allow our emotions to cause us to act out of character and be tossed *to and fro* by *every wind and doctrine.* We, as Believers, must be emotionally stable and secure so that we can grow and achieve the things God has promised us. We must never allow **emotional turmoil** caused by **fear**, **grief**, **betrayer**, **pain** or **abuse** stagnant our Christian growth. We must *cast off emotional distress,* by renewing our minds with God's **Word. (Romans12:1, 2)**

Ways a Believer can renew his or her mind is through church attendance, bible study, meditating upon the Word of God and through fasting and prayer. When a Christian diligently do these things; he or she will no longer use the excuse: *The devil made me do it.*

My brother and sister, let us not allow our **soul** to be an adversary to our spiritual growth, but let us train our **soul** to obey and hearken to our **born-again spirit man** so that we may **walk in the Spirit** from *victory to VICTORY...* and from *glory to GLORY...*

Exposing The Devil

rlshepherdjr@yahoo.com

901-652-3545

You can contact us by writing to:

Robert L. Shepherd Ministries

P.O. Box 40683

Memphis, TN 38174

CHAPTER 2

THE LOVE OF GOD

(A Poem)

For the love of man, Christ died on a cross--
In hope, that no man would be eternally lost.
In agony He hung there, as He bled and died
For man's lust, greed, rebellion and pride.
As Christ blood ran down while he hung on the tree--
It ran down to cover the sins of
wretches, like you and like me.
It ran down to wash us whiter than snow.
It ran down to punch hell with a *mighty* deathblow.

For the love of man, our Savior bled--
Conquered hell and rose from the dead.
And gave to repentant souls the crimson key;
That opens the Celestial Gate to Eternity.
For the love of man, Christ came to the earth--
Entered the womb of a virgin; and
as a man, He was birthed.
He experienced the sufferings of men,
now as our High Priest, He pleads,
And is touched by the feelings of our infirmities.
For God so loved the world, He gave
His Only Begotten Son-
To purchase repentant souls back........
The Victory is Won!!!

By Robert L. Shepherd Jr.

GOD'S LOVE FOR MAN FROM THE BEGINNING

In **Genesis**, the **Book of Beginnings**, Moses records God as the Creator of the heaven and earth:

1. In the beginning God created the heaven and the earth. 2. And the earth was without form, and void; and darkness was upon the face of the deep. And the Spirit of God moved upon the face of the waters. (Genesis 1:1-2)

From these two verses I have quoted, astute biblical scholars have developed what they have term: **the gap theory.** Verse one states that *"In the beginning God created the heaven and the earth."* **Knowing the fact** that *God is a God of order*, these biblical scholars suggest that God, in verse one, created a perfect world—*a world of order*...and that, subsequently, between verses one and two, something chaotic and drastic happened in the earth. Verse two states that"...*the world was without form, and void; and darkness was upon the face of the deep...*"

Some proponents of **the gap theory** teaches and believes that Satan, when he was kicked out of heaven following the period verse one of Genesis occurred, entered the earth (territory which he was very familiar with because he had once according to Ezekiel 28, *walked* in the Garden of Eden) and, in his disgust and wrath, wrecked havoc upon the pre-Adamic world...deceiving, corrupting and destroying the *inhabiting creatures* thereof by flooding the globe with water and darkness.

The gap theory implies or suggests that many uncountable years transpire between *verse one* and *two* and during *verse one and verse two* of the first chapter of Genesis.

If the gap theory is correct and I believe that it is, the earth is older than the six thousands years which some theologians believe and teach it to be. Scientist could be right by believing the earth is millions or billions of years old. Some of the fossils of prehistoric animals could also be millions or billions of years old.

In verse 3 of the first chapter of Genesis, God begins a restoration project in the earth. During the first five days, God sets about the work of refurbishing the earth, which according to the gap theory; the devil had flooded and plunged into chaos. God divides the waters from the dry land and creates the smiling shiny simmering sensational sun to rule the day and the amazing majestic marvelous meticulous moon along with shimmering sensational stars to shine, twinkle and govern the night. God then sets about the task of replenishing the earth with animals both great and small—from microorganisms and insects to giraffes and whales. From the dust of the ground, He created elephants and bears, tigers and lions, hippopotamus and fish, cattle and the fowl of the air and innumerable of other creatures. Then God smiled upon His creations and observed, *"…It was very good."*

*"And God said, Let us make man in our image, after our likeness: and let them have dominion over the fish of the sea, and over the fowl of the air, and over the cattle, and over all the earth, and over every creeping thing that creepeth upon the earth. And God blessed them, and God said unto them, Be fruitful and multiple, and **replenish** the earth, and subdue it: and have dominion over the fish of the sea, and over the fowl of the air, and over every living thing that moveth upon the earth."*
Genesis 1:26-27

God already had the companionship of angels and a world of animals that He had created, but He wanted something more. God now desired and wanted a creature dissimilar to the animals and his *servants* the angels...one whom He could relate to more intimately and fellowship with more personally, in the cool of the day. **God wanted a creature more like Himself**: One whom he could laugh with, talk to and call *"friend"*. So on the sixth day, God personally stooped down in the earth and scooped up earthen clay tenderly in His big bronzed hands and pensively, patiently, excitingly and insightfully molded Himself a creature in His Own Image and Likeness and for His own pleasure and breathed into **man** life. Then God blessed man and all He had created: *"And God saw every thing that he had made, and, behold, it was very good. And evening and the morning were the sixth day."*
Genesis 1:31

In verse 27 of the first chapter of Genesis, God tells man to be fruitful and multiply and **replenish** the earth. Why did God use the word **replenish**? Was there a creature *somewhat* *like man* that had once existed in the earth before the devil plunged the world into a watery grave of chaos and darkness? I honestly believe that God has given me the answer to this question, but I do not want to wax too deep and confound and confuse my readers. Besides, that is another topic for another book. This book is about the ***love of God***.

I know that sometimes God gives me profound insights and revelations in my books that many of my readers cannot in a brief moment digest or comprehend...but what I say causes them to pause and think and search the scriptures for themselves...and plunder the thought that what I'm saying (even though they do not presently understand) could and may actually be true.

All of my revelations, though unfamiliar to some they may be, are based on the 66 books of the Canon and on other Five-Fold ministry teachings...I do not use the apocryphal texts.

Also, I give scriptures with my insights so that ministers and bible students can examine the views I pose by the word of God, and hopefully, with the help of the Holy Spirit, come up with the sound and correct conclusion for themselves...

God can give individuals *personal revelations*; but <u>there can be no</u> *private interpretation* of the Scriptures.

I will not confound my readers in this book with philosophical and deep concepts but I will delve deeply into the Word of God and examine the complexity and profundity of God's Love. By the guidance of the Holy Ghost, I will do it with simplicity so that even readers that are new to the

Word of God and biblical terminologies and precepts, may clearly perceive, comprehend and understand the love of our Heavenly Father.

As I stated earlier, God created a man in His own Image and Likeness. *"And the Lord God planted a garden eastward in Eden; and there he put the man whom he had formed. And out of the ground made the Lord God to grow every tree that is pleasant to the sight, and good for food; the tree of life also in the midst of the garden, and the tree of knowledge of good and evil... And the Lord God took the man, and put him into the garden of Eden to dress it and to keep it. And the Lord God commanded the man, saying, Of every tree of the garden thou mayest freely eat: But of the tree of the knowledge of good and evil, thou shalt not eat of it: for in the day that thou eatest thereof thou shalt surely die."* Genesis 2:8-9, 15-17

"And the Lord God said, it is not good that the man should be alone; I will make him an help meet for him....And the Lord God caused a deep sleep to fall upon Adam, and he slept: and he took one of his ribs, and closed up the flesh instead thereof; And the rib, which the Lord God had taken from man, made he a woman, and brought her unto the man. And Adam said, This is now bone of my bones, and flesh of my flesh: she shall be called Woman, because she was taken out of Man. Therefore shall a man leave his father and his mother and shall cleave unto his wife: and they shall be one flesh. And they were both naked, the man and his wife, and were not ashamed." Genesis 2:18, 21-25

God created Adam and Eve and gave them access to eat of every tree of the garden except one: **The tree of the**

knowledge of good and evil. *"And out of the ground made the Lord God to grow every tree that is pleasant to the sight and good for food..."*

Adam and Eve were surrounded in the garden by the serene blustering sounds of life: the quacking of the dancing ducks, the melodious duets of the whistling birds, the croaking of the flecked frogs, the humming of the busy bumble bees, the mooing of the colorful cows, the roaring of the large lazy lions, the growling of the big brown bears, the laughing of the happy hyenas, the hooting of the wise owls; and from numerous of other creatures, an *assorted ensemble* of soul-inspiring notes that only God could have wrote.

In the Garden of Eden there was no death...Life echoed and flourished everywhere!

The endless source of food for the man and the animals in the **gorgeous predominant-green multicolored garden** were the <u>invigorating vegetation,</u> and the <u>opulent and tantalizing fruit of the trees,</u> and <u>milk</u> and <u>honey</u> from the cattle and the bees.

Adam and Eve, newlyweds, naked and in love, roamed through the garden hand and hand, smiling and staring into each other's sparkling eyes as they for the first time, ate of the exotic and delectable fruits while skipping, laughing, and enjoying the animals and the amazing and spectacular greenery of the beautiful garden God had placed them in.

In the cool of the day, God would visit Adam and Eve. With a smile as bright as the noon-day sun beaming from His face, He would walk with them (as love and joy radiated from the essence of His vast Being) through the garden, holding their hand--fellowshipping and laughing with them and teaching them of the wonders of heaven and earth and of the eternal joys of an endless life; telling them stories of distant galaxies and of infinite universes they had not yet seen or explored...He would tell them of *great* and *greater things* they would later experience and admire as eternity, having no end, unwearyingly rolled on.

The angels, whom The Triune-Being God created, could only serve the role as servants, but now God had a friend--someone He could relate intimately too and someone who could love, serve and relate to Him, *as a son to a Father.*

Oh! How God cherish and loved this new creature He had created in His own Likeness and Image and for His own pleasure.

Oh, how much God delighted in the fellowship of man and being in man's presence!

But silently, lurking in the shadows, perched atop the tree of the knowledge of good and evil was the fallen-angel, Satan, flamboyantly disguised in the beautiful and multi-color form of a serpent, waiting...waiting...waiting patiently on the opportune moment to tempt, allure and bereft man of his dominion and birthright as ruler of the earth.

But more dirty, diabolic, disastrous and dastardly than usurping man of his dominion of the earth, the devil was waiting on the opportunity to allure **man** eternally into the bottomless dark pit of the **Kingdom of Death** and separate

man from the unlimited perpetual life and intimate light and love of his Creator and God.

"Now the serpent was more subtil than any beast of the field which the Lord God had made And he said unto the woman, Yea, hath God said, Ye shall not eat of every tree of the garden? And the woman said unto the serpent, We may eat of the fruit of the trees of the garden: But of the fruit of the tree which is in the midst of the garden, God hath said, Ye shall not eat of it, neither shall ye touch it, lest ye die. And the serpent said unto the woman, Ye shall not surely die: God doth know that in the day ye eat thereof, then your eyes shall be opened, and ye shall be as gods, knowing good and evil. And when the woman saw that the tree was good for food, and that it was pleasant to the eyes, and a tree to be desired to make one wise, she took of the fruit thereof, and did eat, and gave also unto her husband with her; and he did eat. And the eyes of them both were opened, and they knew that they were naked; and they sewed fig leaves together, and made themselves aprons." Genesis 3:1-7.

God created Adam and Eve without ***sin-consciousness***. They did not need it. They only *knew* and *exhaled-out* and *breathe-in* the goodness and love of God. There was no guilt, guile, greed, bitterness, selfishness, shame, pride, dishonesty, hatred or evil in his or her nature. They did not know the **devil** and **evil**—they only knew **Good** and **God**.

Satan really had nothing **good** to offer them. He only--***with malice, forethought and intent***--offered them evil things to trick them out of their birthright and caused them to be punished by a **Good and Just God** whom is sworn and obligated by His very nature to judge transgressions and backup every Word that proceeds from His mouth.

God had warned them that the day they ate of the tree of the knowledge of good and evil they would *surely die*. Since they did not heed to His warning, it had now happened to them accordingly. Like lifeless-emotional zombies, they had spasmodic movement but they were now spiritually dead; dazed and confused as they frantically and fearfully wandered through the garden. Spiritual death enveloped them, causing their once-bright visions to dim and focus on darkness and death. Through the *Needle* of **The lust of the flesh, the lust of the eyes and the pride of life** the drug of evil penetrated their veins with sin and as it circulated through their bodies, their souls became sick and weak, inebriated by the intoxicating influence of paranoia and fear. Now, for the very first time, they realized they were naked. Focusing on their nakedness; shame and fear forced them to devise a feeble attempt to cover up themselves...Thus from fig leaves, they made for themselves aprons.

Embarrassed and ashamed, and fearing the soon approaching voice and penetrating eyes and *brightness* of the loving God whom they had betrayed, they hid themselves among the darkness and denseness of the trees.

While all of this was happening, God stood in the bright light of Eternity with rivers of tears flowing from His eyes. God wanted Adam and Eve to willingly keep His commandments and love Him—to love Him not out of fear but out of allegiance; to love Him because of His goodness and because He was God…but they had failed.

But God was not taken aback or surprised by Adam and Eve's rebellion against Him. God is Immutable, Omniscience, Omni-present and Eternal. He exists in the past, in the presence and in the future at the same time. Watching from Eternity, even before the foundation of the world, He had seen their treasonous act and had initiated a plan for their redemption. It was a costly plan…a plan that would require the shedding of blood…***something and Someone would have to die***.

Adam and Eve, having partaken of the forbidden fruit, now for the very first time, became blameful, selfish and self-conscious as the poisonous drug of the ***fruit of evil*** penetrated their being, allowing the spirit of fear to grasps them tighter as they felt their bodies being sapped and changed under the ***hypnotic potion*** of **Sin and Evil**. They didn't realize what was happening to them but they *were aging…and dying*. Now, they remembered the wise and kindly advice spoken by their compassionate and loving Creator: *"And the Lord God commanded the man, saying, Of every tree of the garden thou mayest freely eat: But of the tree of the knowledge of good and evil, thou shalt not eat of it:* ***for in the day that thou eatest thereof thou shalt surely die****."* Genesis 2:16-17

When they partook of the forbidden fruit, spiritual death immediately overshadowed them and their souls became contaminated by the fruit of evil. Confused, scared and alone, and for the very first time spiritually severed from the ever-present communion with the compassionate warmth and comforting luminosity of **The Spirit of Light,** Adam and Eve sought the darkness of the shade of the trees as they heard God approaching to fellowship with them…Apprehensively and with presentiment, and with great fear and foreboding, they quietly lingered in the darkness, dreading their ritual routine walk with their Creator in the cool of the day.

They hid in the shadows. Yet from God's omniscient vantage point of Eternity, He clearly saw them and He stepped down from the third heaven into the garden to help them. He wanted to help. He was hoping that they would come out of the dark shadows of hiding and rush to Him for help when they heard the sound of His approaching, but they did not. They continued to hide from Him—paralyzed by sin, shame and in fear. *"And they heard the voice of the Lord God walking in the garden in the cool of the day: and Adam and his wife hid themselves from the presence of the Lord God amongst the trees of the garden. And the Lord God called unto Adam, and said unto him, Where art thou?"* (Genesis 3: 8-9)

"ADAM! ADAM! *Where are you?"* God voiced echoed and reverberated through the garden. Apprehensively, Adam and Eve came out of the shadows and fearfully approached God. Then Adam said, *"…I heard thy voice in the garden, and I was afraid, because I was naked; and I hid myself."* Why did Adam give this answer for his reluctance to approach his Creator and Friend? Why did Adam not come clean and admit before God, his wife and the devil that he had sinned against God and partaken of the forbidden fruit?

Did Adam believe that God did not know what he and his spouse had done?

God being patience with **man** asked him two other questions in response to the reply Adam had given him to the first question. God wanted to get to the root of the problem--He wanted Adam to come clean: *"And He said, Who told thee that thou wast naked? Hast thou eaten of the tree, whereof I commanded thee that thou shouldest not eat?"* (Genesis 3:11b)

Now Adam can no longer, with white lies, shade the truth—he must come clean—but yet, because of the bewitching effect of the *selfishness of evil* caused by the intoxicating drug of the forbidden fruit, Adam, under the mind-altering influence of sin, passes the blame onto his wife in a final attempt to present himself innocent before God.

"And the man said, The woman whom thou gavest to be with me, she gave me of the tree, and I did eat." Genesis 3:12

(NOTE: This verse denotes the first precursor of accusation, disloyalty, distrust, disagreement and disunity between marital spouses. Before Adam and Eve ate the fruit, they were one...they worked together, they laughed together and their thoughts were pure thoughts of oneness--of holiness and unity...of mutual care and concern for each other's welfare and well-being.)

After HE finishing questioning Adam, God turned to the woman to hear of her excuse for disobeying Him and eating the forbidden fruit. *"And the Lord God said unto the woman, What is this that thou hast done? And the woman said, the serpent beguiled me, and I did eat."* (Genesis 3:13) The woman's excuse is the same blame shifting and classic excuse we use today and Flip Wilson made so famous in the 1970's: *"The devil made me do it."*

The wages of sin is death: *spiritual separation from God.* And now, God must judge the man and woman but He, because of His great love for them, tempers His punishment with *Mercy.* When issuing out man's punishment, God immediately initiates His plan of redemption to restore His *beloved* back unto Himself so that **man** could once again fellowship, commune and enjoy a intimate relationship with Him in the cool of the day...throughout *All Eternity.*

In verse 15 of the third chapter of Genesis, while pronouncing judgment upon that old serpent, the devil, God prophesizes and foretells of the virgin birth and the coming Messiah that would one day crush the serpent's head and bring the devil's dominion in the earth to an end. *"And I will put enmity between thee and the woman, and between thy seed and her seed; and it shall bruise thy head, and thou shall bruise his heel."*

Adam and Eve, now naked and impoverished by sin and shame, attempts to cover themselves by the act of gathering fig leaves and wrapping them around their naked bodies. Even though now, they have covered their flesh, their **souls** (minds, wills and emotions) are still bare and exposed to the tormenting taunts of the terrorizing serpent whom they-- after having partaken of the fruit and having acquired the **knowledge of evil**, now clearly see as their enemy and the ugly malevolence creature he really is. The fig leaves are not enough to cover them **wholly** (body, soul and spirit) and give them peace…God knows this. **Without the shedding of blood there is no remission of sin.**

The prophet Isaiah says in the book of Isaiah, chapter 53 and verses one through six: *"Who hath believed our report? And to whom is the arm of the Lord revealed? For he shall grow up before him as a tender plant, and as a root out of a dry ground: he hath no form nor comeliness; and when we shall see him, there is no beauty that we should desire him. He is despised and rejected of men: a man of sorrows, and acquainted with grief: and we hid as it were our faces from him; he was despised, and we esteemed him not. Surely he hath **borne our griefs**, and **carried our sorrows**: yet we did esteem him stricken, smitten of God, and afflicted. But he was **wounded for our transgressions**, he was **bruised for our iniquities: the chastisement of our peace was upon him**: and **with his stripes we are healed.** All we like sheep have gone astray; we have turned every one to his own way; and **the Lord hath laid on him the iniquity of us all**."*

Isaiah 53:10-11 proclaims, *"Yet it pleased the Lord to bruise him; he hath put him to grief: when thou shalt **make his soul an offering for sin**, he shall see his seed, he shall prolong his days, and the pleasure of the Lord shall prosper in his hand. **He shall see of the travail of his soul, and shall be satisfied**: by his knowledge shall my righteous servant justify many; for **he shall bear their iniquities**."*

In the above verses, the Prophet Isaiah spoke of the coming Messiah that would one day enter the earth to shed His blood to cover and bare the burdens of **man's** sin. Adam and Eve now stood in the Garden of Eden with their bodies wrapped in fig-leaves but they were spiritually and soulically naked and exposed to the serpent's venom and God's wrath... Adam and Eve needed a better covering than the one they had made... *Immediately*, and God knew it!

For the very first time, in the history of man, blood would have to be spilled. For without bloodshed (death) there could be no *remission* or *pardon* for sin.

God, with his own hands, took the life of one of his precious animals so that He could clothe and protect the man and woman He so greatly loved. *"Unto Adam also and to his wife did the Lord God make coats of skins, and clothed them."* Genesis 3:21

Readers, God's love for **man** is so great! His heart's desire is that none should perish but that all men and women would come to him for repentance and allow Him to hold them in His Arms of grace and mercy and give them rest.

"Come!" He beckons. *"Come unto me, all ye that labour and are heavy laden, and I will give you rest. Take my yoke upon you and learn of me: for I am meek and lowly in heart: and ye shall find rest unto your souls. For my yoke is easy, and my burden is light"* Matthew 11:28-30

Through the soul-gates of **the lust of the flesh**, **the lust of the eyes** and **the pride of life**, the spirit of sin entered and contaminated the earth with its deadly virus as it germinated and spread from the **fruit of the knowledge of good and evil** into the blood streams and genes of Adam and his wife and children. When Adam and Eve had sexual intercourse and produce children, the contaminating virus of this venereal disease infested their sons and daughters.

Unlike the **AIDS** virus of today, there was not a medicine that the woman could take during her pregnancy to impede this deadly disease from contaminating her baby and shortening its life. Nor was there a mass inoculation that men could take to cure them of this **dreadful disease of sin**.

The cure for the disease of sin was one that could only be administered individually. Every boy and girl that came into the world through Adam and Eve loins would have to go to Jesus, the **Great Physician**, to receive the cure for themselves.

The cure was costly. Over time, the cure would cost the lives of millions and millions of animals through daily sacrifices on the altar of repentance. But the blood of those innocent animals would only momentarily safeguard and shield **repentant man** in his filthy garments from the wrath and judgment of a Holy and Just God.

Under the Old Testament, once yearly, the High Priest would cautiously enter behind the purple veil of the **Holy of Holies** to offer up unto God a special annual blood sacrifice. This too was only a temporary fix for sin.

The Hebrew children had other **offerings** and **rituals** they performed to gain favor with God but all of their sacrifices were only a *shadow* and a *type*. (Read Exodus, Deuteronomy and Leviticus). It would take more than the blood of animals… the blood of animals could not permanently abate God's wrath and judgment or satisfy as a permanent propitiation for **man's** sin. Animal blood was only a temporary fix.

The ultimate sacrifice and price that would have to be paid for man's **sin-cure** would be the **Blood of Jesus, the sacrifice of** God's Only Begotten Son. On a rugged wooded cross atop the hill of Calvary, beyond the gates of Jerusalem, our Lord Jesus Christ would purchase our **sin-cure** and redeem us back unto Himself by suffering and shedding His Own precious Blood...**The Son of God had to die.** *God so loved the world, He gave his only begotten Son so that whosoever believed on Him would not perish but have everlasting life.*

The first time Adam and Eve had seen the spilling of blood, in death, was when they saw God kill an animal to cover their nakedness and atone for their sins.

Adam and Eve, as time moved forward, conceived and bare children. They delighted in the miracles of holding these little creatures in their arms which they had, through their own flesh, given life unto...they gazed in awe and amazement as these new souls entered the world and took their first breath.

But one day, Adam and Eve would have to go into a field and stare down upon the bloody body of their second-born son, Abel, whom had been killed by, Cain, their first-born.

As they funeralized Abel...They wept.

From their own conscience and from the pit of hell, fiery darts of guilt and condemnation bombarded *the core of their souls*. They were to blame. Accepting the blame, Adam and Eve wept the more.

God, looking over the balcony of Heaven, wept with them. He wanted to reach out and touch them and once again encircle them in His big strong arms and console them, but He could not. Sin had separated **man** from His God and God from **man**.

For the devil, the fallen angels and the demons, there can never be remission of sin; but for **man** there *was* and *is* yet hope. Men, such as Enoch, walked with God and obeyed Him and obtained life. But many of the men and women in the earth before the flood would not heed God's voice and they continued in rebellion against Him.

One day, God spoke to Noah, His servant, and told him to build an Ark and to warn the people to come into the Ark of safety because He was going to destroy the earth.

God's love for man compelled Noah to preach to men and women for a hundred and twenty years, warning them of the earth's pending destruction and inviting them to come to God. Yet they would not listen.

Finally the day of destruction came and the water fell, submerging and drowning the earth. Men, women, boys and girls were wailing, moaning, cursing, praying, crying out and beating upon their chests and upon the Ark, but there was nothing God could do...*for the wages of sin is death*...and sin was being judged. ***Jesus wept***.

Only the eight people that obeyed God and entered the Ark were saved from the wages of sin.

Adam and Eve's eight descendants (Noah and his family) would survive and be fruitful and multiply and once again, *replenish* the earth.

But the virus of sin, lying dormant momentarily--through man would revitalize itself.

As Noah and his family multiplied and spread throughout the earth, the infectious germ of the poisonous fruit that their ancestors had eaten also extended in them and among them and rampantly grew.

On the very first bite, when Adam took of the forbidden fruit, the virus of evil like mist in the wind, hovered through the air spreading the deadly curse of sin through the garden… to the animals and to the vegetation…and throughout all the earth and among every creature upon it.

Now the whole *creation*, chaotic, wild, rampant and out of tune with God, groans…and longs for man's redemption and the *"manifestation of the **sons of God"***.

(See Romans chapter 8:18-25) God, now looking from the glorious **Balcony of Eternity**, longs to restore men and women back unto Him so they can (like Adam and Eve in the beginning) once again fellowship with Him and enjoy His companionship in the cool of the day and bathe unceasingly in the sunshine and warmth of His **Eternal Embrace, Everlasting Life** and **Endless Love.**

Hosanna! Hosanna! Let us resound Infinite praises and shout Eternal Hallelujahs to our Lord Jesus Christ, the True and Living God, for His great Love!!!

THE LOVE OF
KINSMEN REDEEMERS

"And when the people saw that Moses delayed to come down out of the mount, the people gathered themselves together unto Aaron, and said unto him, Up, make us gods, which shall go before us for as for this Moses, the man that brought us up out of the land of Egypt, we wot not what is become of him. And Aaron said unto them, Break off the golden earrings, which are in the ears of your wives, of your sons, and of your daughters, and bring them unto me. And all the people brake off the golden earrings which were in their ears, and brought them unto Aaron. And he received them at their hand, and fashioned it with a graving tool, after he had made it a molten calf: and they said, These be thy gods, O Israel, which brought thee up out of the land of Egypt. And when Aaron saw it, he built an altar before it; and Aaron made proclamation, and said, Tomorrow is a feast to the Lord. And they rose up early on the morrow, and offered burnt offerings, and brought peace offerings; and the people sat down to eat and to drink, and rose up to play. And the Lord said unto Moses, Go, get thee down; for thy people, which thou broughtest out of the land of Egypt, have corrupted themselves: They have turned aside quickly out of the way which I commanded them: they have made them a molten calf, and have worshipped it, and have sacrificed thereunto, and said, These be thy gods, O Israel, which have brought thee up out of the land of Egypt. And the

Lord said unto Moses, I have seen this people, and, behold, it is a stiffnecked people: **Now therefore let me alone that my wrath may wax hot against them, and that I may consume them: and I will make of thee a great nation.** *And Moses besought the Lord his God, and said, Lord why doth thy wrath wax hot against thy people, which thou hast brought forth out of the land of Egypt with great power, and with a mighty hand? Wherefore should the Egyptians speak, and say, For mischief did he bring them out, to slay them in the mountains, and to consume them from the face of the earth? Turn from thou fierce wrath, and repent of this evil against thy people. Remember Abraham, Isaac, and Israel, thy servants, to whom thou swarest by thine own self, and saidst unto them, I will multiple your seed as the stars of heaven, and all this land that I have spoken of will I give unto your seed, and they shall inherit it forever. And the Lord repented of the evil which he thought to do unto his people."*
Exodus 32:1-14

"And Moses returned unto the LORD, and said, Oh, this people have sinned a great sin, and have made them gods of gold. Yet now, ***if thou wilt forgive their sin--; and if not, blot me, I pray thee, out of the book which thou hast written****."*
(Exodus 32:31-32)

The Oxford American Dictionary defines **kinsman** as: a *blood relative* or *someone relative (in someway or another) to someone else.*

In the O.A.D. **redeem** means: *to recover or buy back (a thing or person) by payment or by taking some decisive action.* **Therefore, a *kinsman redeemer* is one who can**

in someway *relate* to an individual or a group of people that are imprisoned, impoverished or in trouble and who has the compassion, capacity or cash to intercede for the unfortunate *individual* or group of *people* and rescue or bail them out.

In this chapter I will speak of several kinsmen redeemers, whom being provoked by love and love alone, and at the expense of their own safety, life and material possessions, interceded and stood in the gap to rescue or purchase back <u>an individual</u> or <u>a group of people</u> whom were related to them by either; covenant, race, ethnicity or faith.

I will begin with Moses, as he stood face to face with God in the wilderness of Sinai and demanded that God not kill His people--the Hebrew (Israelites) children.

In Exodus chapter 19, the Hebrew children had stood in awe beneath Mount Sinai trembling and fearing for their lives as bellows of fire filled the air with thick dark clouds accompanied by thunder and lightning and loud trumpet sounds, and as the voice of God, like many rushing waters, roared *rampantly* and riveted through the crowd; producing within the camp Godly terror, reverence and respect.

In Exodus chapter 20, God, through Moses, had given the Hebrew children the Ten Commandments and they agree *among themselves,* before Moses and God that they would honor and keep the sacred commandments. They knew the consequences if they didn't keep them would be righteous retribution which would be in some cases death.

In Exodus chapter 31, Moses goes up unto Mount Sinai to receive the commandments personally written by the finger of God on tables of stone. Moses stays on the mountaintop for forty days and forty nights...The Israelites grow weary— their patience wears thin and rumors start spreading around and about the camp that Moses is dead. *"If Moses was alive, he would have been back by now"* they reasoned and complained. *"What will we do now without Moses or a god to lead us?"*

In the verses, we read from the book of Exodus to begin this chapter, we observed a mob of people as they approached Aaron, ***insisting that he make them a god***...Aaron wasted no time. He gathered up all the golden earring in the camp and he made them a ***golden calf.***

Earlier, on their journey to the Promised Land (in Exodus chapter 20), the Children of Israel had promised the God of Abraham, Isaac and Jacob that they would obey Him and Him alone. It has been less than forty days and these same people, in Exodus chapter 32, have abandoned their promises and forsaken, **JEHOVAH**, the true and living God. **How could they so soon forget God and the promises they had made to Him?**

You and I know...we have done the same thing or something similar to what these Hebrew children did. We too have made promises to God and in the passage of time broken or forsaken them.

Aaron, the high priest, without hesitation, went alone with their demands as he absentmindedly pushed the Living and invisible God of Abraham, Isaac and Jacob aside to fashion for the Hebrew congregation an idol god of gold.......

Not Aaron too?

God had supernaturally delivered the Israelites out of the hands of Pharaoh and had made a highway through the Red Sea so that they could, without drowning, bogging in mud or even getting wet, cross over safely to the other side. God had also miraculously fed them in the wilderness with manna--bread from heaven!

Only **JEHOVAH**, the true and living God could have done the miracles in their lives, which they had experienced in Egypt and were daily witnessing in the wilderness. **How could they forget HIM?**

God now decided to forget and disown them; shifting the responsibility and guardianship of the Israelites to Moses... He calls them Moses' people: *"thy people".*

God was mad...!

He was angry and His cauldron of wrath was full and ready to boil over, run down and consume and melt the Hebrew Children carcasses amidst the desert's sand in the fiery concoction of His burning wrath. **God wanted to kill them all**! *"And the Lord said unto Moses, Go, get thee down; for **thy people**, which **thou broughtest out** of the land of Egypt, have corrupted themselves; They have turned aside quickly out of the way which I commanded them: they have made them a molten calf, and have worshipped it, and have sacrificed thereunto, and said, These be thy gods, O Israel, which have brought thee up out of the land of Egypt. And the Lord said unto Moses, I have seen* *this people, and, behold, it is a stiffnecked people: Now therefore let me alone, that my wrath may wax hot against them, and that I may consume them: and I will make of thee a great nation."*

The Hebrew children needed a Kinsman Redeemer—someone who would at the risk of his own life and safety love them enough to stand in the gap between them and an angry and Holy God and intercede. **Up stepped Moses!**

Through fellowship and face-to-face-like intimacy with God, Moses had learned and knew that *"the effectual fervent prayer of a righteous man availeth much."* James 5:16

Moses stood in the gap, and with passion and fervency, he began to *talk with God* on behalf of a sinful people.

But God wanted Moses to *shut up* and *stand back* out of the way so He could *kill* them all. God even promised Moses that if he would just only clear the path, He would kill everybody in the camp and He would raise up a great nation from Moses' seed. But Moses' love for God and his relatives was Greater than his desire for personal power or achievements... or even his own life. **Noooo!** Moses interceded! **God, you can't do this!**

Moses stood boldly before Almighty God and told God what HE couldn't do. **Had the heat of the desert's sun overcome Moses? Had Moses lost his mind?**

This was not absentmindedness, madness or audacity on Moses' part, but perfect love in him had conquered all fear. (I John 4:18)

Moses pleaded on: *"Wherefore should the Egyptians speak, and say, For mischief did he bring them out, to slay them in the mountains and to consume them from the face of the earth? Turn from thy fierce wrath, and repent of this evil against thy people."*

Moses points out to God that if He destroyed the Israelites, the Egyptians were going to talk about it and insist that JEHOVAH was a *mischievous* and *mean* God who brought the Hebrews out of Egypt only to annihilate them in the wilderness. So Moses pleaded that God, for reputation-sake, relent.

But this did not stop God or appease His wrath. God was still headed towards Moses to destroy the Hebrew Children from off the face of the earth...

Moses held his ground and stood firm in the gap...**Yet, God kept coming**.

Fervent and Determined, Moses was not quiet through or willing to give up in his intercessory fight with God for the lives of his kinsmen. The Cosmic poker game for the lives of the Hebrew Children seemed hopeless and loss, but Moses had one more card up his sleeve so to speak...it was an **Ace of Heart**. Moses now would use it to penetrate the very Spirit and essence of God: **Moses reminded God of His Word.**

Moses said. *"Remember Abraham, Isaac and Israel, thy servants, to whom thou swarest by thine own self, and saidst unto them, I will multiply your seed as the stars of heaven, and all this that I have spoken of will I give unto your seed, and they shall inherit it forever."* At those words, God stopped. His anger instantly abated and He repented of the evil which he thought to do unto ***His*** people.

I could not talk about **Kinsmen Redeemers** without making a slight reference to the Book of Ruth and to the story about how Boaz redeemed Ruth, from **a life of poverty** *to* **wealth**, from **incest** *to* **Beauty** and how he redeemed her mother-in-law, Naomi, from (**bitterness** *to* **pleasant and sweet)**, on their return from the land of Moab (a place of backsliding) to **Bethlehem-Juda** (*home and house of bread*).

Boaz's love for Ruth caused him to be willing to give up his own birthright and allow the *child* that he and his *beloved* would someday birth to take on the name and lineage of Naomi's deceased husband Elimelech and his sons. **What a sacrifice!** But love compelled and drove him to do it…and Boaz did it with joy and delight because he loved Ruth, the Moabitess.

Jesus said, *"Greater love hath no man than this, that a man lay down his life for his friends."* John 15:13

All Kinsmen Redeemers must give up or sacrifice something.

Redeemers must love something greater than their possessions and greater than themselves…and they must be willing to sacrifice their goods, reputations, security of even their own lives for the object of their love and affection.

Our ultimate Kinsman Redeemer, like Moses, would stand in the gap between sinful man and an angry God and He would plead man's case—not on the *merits* or *goodness* of man. Not even on man's innocence (man was guilty)…Christ would plead man's case entirely on His own merit and on the power of His own Blood.

The book of Hosea tells us of another Kinsman Redeemer. This book is a love story...in fact, it is the greatest Love Story ever told.

Shakespeare' **Romeo and Juliet** is a great love story but it is a Tragedy, but the story of Hosea and Gomer is a triumphant love story of Redemption and Salvation. It is a story of a man's unfaltering love for an unfaithful and adulteress woman. The name, *Hosea* or *Hoshea* means <u>Salvation</u>. The name *Gomer* means <u>completion</u>.

The leading man, Hosea, is in love with this sensuous and beautiful feminine creature, Gomer. Hosea is deeply in love with this lady but she does not love or appreciates him or the security he provides, nor the gifts he continuously and faithfully lavish upon her with love and fondness. Gomer's heart and affections (even though she is married to Hosea) are devoted unto other men and the things of the world...she "*whores after other gods.*"

This turbulent love affair between Hosea and Gomer was orchestrated, ordained and recorded by our Soreveign Lord to demonstrate His steadfast love and commitment for His chosen people even when they don't faithfully return His love and loyalty. This love story in the book of **HOSEA** teaches us that God does not believe in divorce...He, in all of His Holiness, is, nevertheless, married to the adulterous filthy back-slider.

Paul tells the Church in Philippi of Macedonia this: "*Grace be unto you, and peace, from God our Father, and from the Lord Jesus Christ. I thank my God upon every remembrance of you, Always in every prayer of mine for you all making request with joy, for your fellowship in the gospel from the first day until now;* **Being confident of this very thing, that he which hath began a good work in you will perform it until the day of Jesus Christ***:"* (Philippians 1:2-6)

Hosea's name means __salvation__ and Gomer's name means __completion__. The *salvation* (deliverance and redemption) that Hosea gave Gomer by marrying and accepting her as His bride would be, *by Hosea's grace and love,* __completed__ in her. Gomer would eventually come to love and adore Hosea, her loving and faithful husband because Hosea first loved her. The Apostle John said in I John 4:19: *"We love him, because he first loved us."*

This universal and perpetual love story begins like this *"… And the Lord said to Hosea, Go, take unto thee a wife of whoredoms and children of whoredoms: for the land hath committed great whoredoms, departing from the lord."* (Hosea 1:2)

Hosea, at God's command, goes forth and married a loose and whorish woman named Gomer and she has children— some which were probably not Hosea's. Hosea falls deeply in love with this woman but this lady does not return Hosea's love and affection. Gomer's love is for other men. She goes out and commits adulteries and whoredoms with other men and become polluted and defiled by adultery and idolatry.

Hosea, speaking as a surrogate for God, tells his children this: *"Plead with your mother, plead: for she is not my wife, neither am I her husband: let her therefore put away her whoredoms out of her sight, and her adulteries from between her breasts; Lest I strip her naked, and set her as in the day that she was born, and make her as a wilderness, and set her like a dry land, and slay her with thirst. And I will not have mercy upon her children; for they be the children of whoredoms. For their mother hath played the harlot: she that conceived them hath done shamefully: for she said, I will go after my lovers, that give me my bread and my water, my wool and my flax, mine oil and my drink. Therefore, behold, I will hedge up thy way with thorns, and make a wall, that she shall not find her paths. And she shall follow after her lovers, but she shall not overtake them; and she shall seek them, but shall not find them:* **then shall she say, I will go and return to my first husband; for then was it better with me than now.** *For she did not know that I gave her corn, and wine, and oil, and multiplied her silver and gold, which they prepared for Baal."* Hosea 2:2-8

"Good understanding giveth favour: but the way of transgressors is hard." (Proverbs 13:15) Gomer eventually learns this verse to be true as she finds herself broken, naked and penniless on the auction block of life…waiting to be bought by the person who would offer the highest bid.

Gomer is no longer the beautiful and exotic woman Hosea married. *Age* and *sin* have stripped Gomer of her beauty and she is now a middle-aged woman, tainted by sin, infirmities, shame and abuse. **Who would buy her?** *What man in his right mind would want her now?*

Gomer needed a Kinsman Redeemer to purchase her off Satan's auction block…One who intimately knew her and could relate to her condition and *be touch by the feelings of her infirmities.* God, once again would softly caress the heart of Hosea, her estranged husband, and send him to her rescue. *"Then said the Lord unto me, Go yet, love a woman beloved of her friend, yet an adulteress, according to the love of the Lord toward the children of Israel, who look to other gods, and love flagons of wine.* **So I bought her to me for fifteen pieces of silver, and for an homer of barley, and an half homer of barley:** *And I said unto her, Thou shalt abide for me many days; thou shalt not play the harlot, and thou shalt not be for another man: So will I also be for thee."* Hosea 3:1-3

God, through Hosea, wooed and romanced Gomer with *soft-talk* to lure her back. Others had used and discarded her but Hosea loved her, unconditionally, and He wanted her back home.

In the following verses God promises Gomer peace, restoration; a bright future and an eternal home. *"Therefore, behold, I will allure her, and bring her into the wilderness, and* **speak comfortably unto her.** *And I will give her her vineyards from thence, and the valley of Achor for a door of hope: and she shall sing there, as in the days of her youth, and as in the day when she came up out of the land of Egypt. And it shall be at that day, saith the Lord, that thou shalt call me Ishi; and shalt call me no more Baali. For I will take away the names of Baalim out of her mouth, and they shall no more be rememberd by their name. And in that day will I make a covenant for them with the beasts of the field, and with the fowls of heaven, and with the creeping things of the ground: and I will break the bow and the sword and the battle out of the earth, and will make them to lie down* *safely.* ___And I will betroth thee unto me for ever; yea, I will betroth thee unto me in righteousness, and in judgment, and in lovingkindness, and in mercies. I will even betroth thee unto me in faithfulness: and thou shalt know the Lord.___ *And it shall come to pass in that day, I will hear, saith the Lord, I will hear the heavens, and they shall hear the earth; And the earth shall hear the corn, and the wine, and the oil; and they shall hear Jezreel. And I will sow her unto me in the earth; and I will have mercy upon her that had not obtained mercy; and I will say to them which were not my people, Thou art my people; and they shall say, Thou art my God."* (Hosea 3:14-23)

This love story of Hosea and Gomer is symbolic of God's love for Israel and His love for us. Like Gomer, we have all gone astray and forsaken the Very One who sustains us and supplies our daily needs and we have gone lusting after other gods. But Christ yet loves us. And like Hosea, He is willing to redeem and purchase us back from the world, but we must allow Him. We must repent of our sins and ask Him to save us and then we must accept Him as our Lord and Redeemer and love Him with all of our heart, our soul, our mind and strength as He has commanded us.

Our Redeemer deserves our love, adoration and respect. ***O COME***, *let us adore Him*!

In the book of Zechariah, the third chapter, the high priest Joshua goes before God in filthy garments. The penalty for a high priest going behind the veil of the Holy of Holies and approaching God inappropriately or in tainted attire was death. Joshua needed an Advocate...Someone whom would stand in the gap for him as he stood in the gap for the people of Judah. The high priest of Judah needed a **High Priest** himself…Joshua needed a **Redeemer.**

Let's read and listen with our *spirit man*, as Zechariah describes this dramatic event that took place in Heaven as it was revealed to him by an angel of the Lord.

"Then he (the messaging angel) *showed me Joshua the high priest standing before the angel of the Lord and Satan standing at his right side to accuse him. The Lord said to Satan, The Lord rebuke you, Satan! The Lord, who has chosen Jerusalem, rebuke you! Is not this man a burning stick snatched from the fire? Now Joshua was dressed in filthy clothes as he stood before the angel. The angel said to those who were standing before him, Take off his filthy clothes. Then he said to Joshua See, I have taken away your sin, and I will put rich garments on you."* Zechariah 3:1-4 NIV

In the above scriptures, the high priest of Judah, in filthy rags, stands before the throne of God. And the devil, serving as prosecutor, is standing on Joshua's right-hand side accusing him of having on unclean garments in the presence of a Righteous and Holy God.

Joshua is in trouble…! What can sedate God's judgment and wrath? The wages of sin is death and nothing unclean can stand before God. Joshua needs a Redeemer and he needs one **FAST…!** Look! On the right-hand side nearest to God, **The Angel of the Lord** is also standing; interceding for the high priest and for the people of Judah.

God, hearing the pleading words of (the Angel of the Lord) His Son, the High Priest and Advocate of heaven, tells

Satan *"The Lord rebuke you, Satan! The Lord, who has chosen Jerusalem, rebuke you!" Is not this man a burning stick snatched from the fire?"*

Our Lord rebukes the devil and informs him that He called and chose Joshua as high priest over the people of Judah and Jerusalem. The Lord goes on to say that He, Himself, snatched Joshua from the ravishing fire of hell and damnation—just as a man would rapidly snatch a precious stick from a burning fireplace to keep it from being totally consumed...Joshua belonged to God.

The reason God could *legally* pardon Joshua in the High Court of Heaven is because Joshua, as high priest, stood before the angel of the Lord with the vessel of the sacrificial substitution-al blood of the Lamb of God. Joshua, although dressed in filthy garments, was covered by the Blood. ***Hallelujah!*** (See Hebrew 4:14-16)

The angel of the Lord, who is undoubtedly the Son of God, said to the holy angelic bailiffs who were stationed in the Court, *"Take off his filthy clothes."* Then the angel of the Lord said, *"See, I have taken away your sin, and I will put rich garments on you."* The angel of the Lord that Zechariah saw was our **Kinsman Redeemer** and **Lord, Jesus Christ**. No one can forgive sins and adorn a filthy man with clean garments but our Savior and Lord

Moses, Boaz, and Hosea were types of Kinsmen Redeemers...these men, out of pure love rescued and redeemed impoverished and desperate souls. One even stood in the gap between sinful man and a Holy God and through intercessory prayer, perseverance and self-sacrifice ceased God's wrath and led souls safely to the Land of Promise. But Joshua, the high priest of Judah, encountered another type of Kinsman Redeemer; a Melchisedec-like High Priest: **Our Lord and Savior Christ Jesus, Himself.**

Our Lord and Savior Jesus Christ was the ultimate High Priest and **Kinsman Redeemer**...He paid the ultimate price. He sacrificially shed His precious Blood on the cross of Calvary and when He ascended to His Heavenly Father, he sprinkled that precious crimson blood upon the Mercy Seat to appease His Father and to redeem men back unto God... For without the shedding of blood, the writer of Hebrews graciously informed us; there can be no remission of sin.

Job said, *"For I know that my **redeemer** liveth, and that he shall stand at the latter day upon the earth: And though after my skin worms destroy this body, yet in my flesh shall I see God."* (Job 19:25)

David exhorted, *"Bless the Lord, O my soul: and all that is within me, bless his holy name. Bless the Lord, O my soul, and forget not all his benefits: Who **forgiveth all thine iniquities**; Who **healeth all thy diseases**; Who **redeemeth** **thy life from destruction**; who **crowneth thee with lovingkindness and tender mercies**; Who **satisfieth thy mouth with good things**; so that thy youth is renewed like the eagle's."* Psalm 103:1-5

GOD'S LOVE DEMONSTRATED THROUGH HIS SON, JESUS

John, the apostle who surnamed himself *"the disciple whom Jesus love"* wrote in his gospel these words: *"For God so loved the world, that he gave his only begotten Son, that whosoever believeth in him should not perish, but have everlasting life. For God sent not his Son into the world to condemn the world; but that the world through him might be saved."* John 3:16-17

John states that God loved **mankind** (the world) so much...God was concerned for the welfare of the _body_, _soul_ and _spirit_ of **man** so much that He took action and **demonstrated His love and devotion**, by giving, as the ultimate sacrifice for **man's** ransom and redemption, the life of His Only Begotten Son.

God sent His Son Jesus Christ from Heaven to Earth to suffer, bleed and die for the salvation and emancipation of the Human Race. When man felled into sin, God could have destroyed **man** or looked aside and left **mankind** to his own end and destruction or left man in the devil's firm diabolical clutches, but God could not. God's love for man was greater than His wrath or indifference...God loved the world so much that He gave the life of His Only Begotten Son to purchase mankind back from the imprisoning steel claws of the **Devious and Deceitful Tyrant**, *the devil*.

As you read this chapter, I pray that you'll clearly and vividly see God's love demonstrated through His Son, Jesus.

As you and I endeavor on the project of reading and writing this book, I also fervently pray that the same love which God so greatly manifested by giving His only **Begotten Son** as a living sacrifice *germinates* and *spreads abroad* in my heart and yours by the Holy Ghost--to the degree that our lives demonstrate to an uncaring and blind world the **extraordinary brilliance** of the sensational *concern*, spectacular *care* and *covering-comforting grace* made available to us by our Loving and Compassionate Creator who made us in *His* Image.

I pray fervently and diligently for the wisdom and insight to surgically and strategically unravel and dissect scriptures that clearly and vividly reveal and communicate the Love that God so passionately and clearly demonstrated for **the human race** when He, with wisdom, forethought and foresight, freely and willingly gave His Son Jesus as a propitiation for the **sin** of the world.

In this chapter, I will take us on a journey through the gospels of Matthew, Mark, Luke and John and we will observe and watch the Son of Man as He walks the shores of Galilee and throughout the Judean coast demonstrating His Heavenly Father's *power and love* for the human race.

We'll look through Christ compassionate eyes, as He gaze upon the sick with an inner longing and conviction to heal them all. And we'll be in reverent awe and silence as we listen to Christ speak with authority and minister to the hurting hordes of humanity as He pass their way teaching and encouraging them to love, trust and obey His Father, Jehovah God, and to love one another.

In this chapter, through the writers of the gospels, I believe that Christ will reveal Himself to us and disclose, as clearly as possible *through a glass darkly*, the incomprehensible and immeasurable love of His Heavenly Father for the Human Race.

God loved the world so much, the gospel writer John declared, that He gave His only Begotten Son as a ransom (or sacrificial offering) to redeem men and women back unto Himself and break the curse of **Sin and Death** which held the throat of **man** firmly in its maddening and tightening grip. If God had not intervened by sending His Son to man's rescue to break the strangle-hold, **Sin and Death** would have thoroughly drained man of life and would have eternally separated **man** from his God and would have everlastingly cloaked him in darkness and transported **man's** body and soul to the lake of fire. For the wages of sin is death...*spiritual darkness and separation from God.*

I pray that God will use this book, **The Power of Love,** to stir and wake us up and to ignite a *fire of praise* under our feet so that we may, united with our brothers and sisters, leap heavenwards with joy to embrace our Lord and Savior Jesus Christ and to worship and adore Him for the great sacrifice He willingly and without reservation made for us when He allowed the puny creatures which He Himself had created to beat, mock, abuse and nail him to a cross so that, by grace through faith, he might save some of those same men and women who so passionately hated, rejected and maltreated him.

"Forgive them Father, for they know not what they do" a marred, battered, bloody and rejected Christ, aching and throbbing with pain, cried out on the cross, interceding for the unrepentant and wretched souls who mocked and crucified Him. Even though these men brutally beat and crucified Christ, Christ wanted His Father to forgive and save them all. **What a demonstration and show of the forgiving and triumphant power of love!** Oh God, give us this type of love so that we will willingly and freely forgive those who abuse, revile, slander and persecute us. Let this same *agape* love from above be shed abroad in our hearts by your Holy Spirit which dwells in the hearts of every Believer. Just as you sent your Son Christ into the earth, send us on a mission of love as we daily go about our task. Let the world see your love demonstrated through us, as we exemplify love one for another and as we weep for the *hurting and lost masses* and compassionately lend a hand to pull some poor wretched soul from the gutters of life to lead them to the cross so that they too can encounter Your *Love.*

Our Lord Jehovah, You are <u>one</u> God. But for the love of the human race, in infinite eternity—in endless eons before the foundation of the world--You strategically revealed and exhibited Yourself in three Persons: **God the Father, God the Son** and **God the Holy Spirit** as the *deliberate* and *eternal* way to redeem repentant man back unto Yourself.

In the very beginning of mankind existence when you made the heavens and the earth and on the sixth day said, *"Let us make man in our own image"* You *was* addressing Yourself in the *Triune Form* of **Father**, **Son** and **Holy Ghost**.

Being Omniscient, You already knew in Your eternal existence, even before the foundation of the world, that man would be separated from You by sin and that it would take the works of You operating as a **Triune Being** to deliver the *fallen creature* You so greatly loved and created in Your Own Image back unto Yourself. Therefore, Your love for degenerate fallen-man caused You to implement a plan which would allow You to simultaneously perform three roles in the redemption of the Human Race; as **God the Father, God the Son** and **God the Holy Ghost**.

Let every man, woman, boy, girl and infant that has breath be appreciated and praise YOU with a joyful noise for Your <u>Triunity</u>! For only You, the True and Living God functioning in Your <u>Triunity</u> could have simultaneously given Your life for us, pardoned us; forgiven, saved and filled us with Your Spirit.

Church, there is but One God. The angelic and demonic world knows this. They look in awe and try to comprehend how a *Just* and *Holy God* would for the love and redemption of mundane man, supernaturally *divide* Himself, yet remain whole and united in the ***Eternal Spiritual sphere of One,*** to perform the triune tasks of **<u>Heavenly Father</u>, <u>Crucified Resurrected Redeeming Son</u>** and **<u>Instructing, Comforting,</u>**

Reproving Holy Ghost.

God *is* one God, as the Orthodox Jews states *firmly, truthfully* and *with conviction*: *"The Lord our God is one God."* **But Lord, what they do not know is this:** You *constitute* and You *are* the Father, Son and Holy Spirit. **The *Son* is in the *Father* and the *Holy Ghost* is in the *Son*…**There is but one God. But in *man's redemption*, **You** perform three roles as **God**, (Father) **Savior** (Son) and **Sin-convicting Comforter and Counselor** (Holy Spirit).

My readers and Jewish friends, our Lord and Savior Christ Jesus, the Son of God who came to earth in the flesh is in essence—not only *equal to*; but He's *totally and completely* **Almighty God.**

When we get to heaven, we will recognize and worship as the angels already do, ***One God.*** The Son, having triumph over every enemy, shall subject Himself to the Father and the Spirit *"that God may be all in all."* Therefore, when we get to heaven we'll see only one God…**All the glory of the Godhead will be revealed in the face of Jesus. *Hallelujah!!!***

On numerous of occasions the word of God speaks of Jesus, as *"God's only Begotten Son"*. The question an inquisitive soul would now ask is this *two-fold* one: **What do *begotten* means** and **when was Christ begotten?** The word ***begotten*** in the Greek language is ***monogenes***, which means: ***only-born*** or ***sole***. The Greek word for ***son*** is ***huios***.

The term *"God's only Begotten Son"* means that Christ became the sole and first human heir of the Godhead, when

He (through the supernatural insemination of the Virgin Mary with the Seed of God by the overshadowing of the Holy Ghost) became flesh (a man) and dwelt among us. The Apostle John beautifully describes this miraculous act like this: *"In the beginning was the Word, and the Word was with God, and the Word was God. The same was in the beginning with God…And the Word was made flesh, and dwelt among us, (and we beheld his glory, the glory as of the only begotten of the Father,) full of grace and truth."* (John 1:1,14)

Paul when exhorting us to exhibit the qualities and virtues of Christ Jesus, spoke of how Christ was **begotten** and took on *"the likeness of men"* in Philippians 2:5-11. *"Let this mind be in you which was also in Christ Jesus:* **Who, being in the form of God, thought it not robbery to be equal with God***: But made himself of no reputation,* ***and took upon him the form of a servant, and was made in the likeness of men:*** *and being found in fashion as a man, he humbled himself, and became obedient unto death, even the death of the cross. Wherefore God also hath highly exalted him, and given him a name which is above every name: That at the name of Jesus every knee should bow, of things in heaven, and things in the earth, and things under the earth; And that every tongue should confess that Jesus Christ is Lord, to the glory of God the Father."*

To restore man back unto God and defeat the devil and his evil horde, Christ had to be born of the flesh and shed His precious blood on the cross. Through this sacrifice of love, He has valiantly and willingly accomplished this task by becoming **God's only Begotten Son,** the **Sacrificial Lamb** and our **soon coming King.**

One day in eternity, very soon, Our Lord Jesus Christ shall submit all to God and the Godhead shall once again become ***all in all***. Let's read the following text: "*Then cometh the end, when he (Christ Jesus) shall have delivered up the kingdom to God, even the Father; when he shall have put down all rule and all authority and power. For he must reign, till he hath put all enemies under his feet. The last enemy that shall be destroyed is death. For he hath put all things under his feet. But when he saith all things are put under him, it is manifest that he is excepted, which did put all things under him. And when all things shall be subdued unto him, then shall the Son also himself be subject unto him that put all things under him, that **God may be all in all.**" (I Corinthians 15:24-28)

When we get to Heaven we will see **one** God in ***the countenance and glory of the face of Jesus***. Revelation 21:22-23 speaks of heaven in this way: "*And I saw no temple therein: for the Lord God Almighty and the Lamb are the temple of it. And the city had no need of the sun, neither of the moon, to shine in it: for the glory of God did lighten it, and the Lamb is the light thereof.*"

In the New Jerusalem which shall descend down from the Third Heaven, there will not be a material building or house like the temple King Solomon built for the Ark of God and for God to dwell in. Instead of a material building the **Godhead** will now abide in a **Tangible Spirit Body.**

In the above text, the Greek word _**naos**_, which means _**temple**_ or _**dwelling place**_ is in the _singular_. This let us know that "..._the Lord God Almighty and the Lamb_" will eternally dwell in <u>one</u> **Tangible Body** (Temple). In heaven there will be order...and no confusion of how to address **3 Deities**. We will not encounter three individuals. **God** (the Father, Son and Holy Spirit) will dwell and reside in **One Temple** and will be **All-In-All.** _Blessed_ be the name of the Lord!

In the gospels of Matthew, Mark, Luke and John, God, in so many spectacular ways, demonstrated His love to the multitudes through His Son Jesus Christ by ministering to them through thought-provoking teachings and through miraculous demonstrations of His compassion and concern. In His **sermon on the mount,** He taught His disciples and the multitudes many wonderful things concerning his enormous empathy and care for _**man**_. Let's focus on Matthew chapter 5, verses 38 through 48 and explore what Christ taught about the immensity of His love in these inspiring and priceless verses.

"_Ye have heard that it hath been said, An eye for an eye, and a tooth for a tooth: But I say unto you, That ye resist not evil: but whoso ever shall smite thee on thy right cheek, turn to him the other also. And if any man will sue thee at the law, and take away thy coat, let him have thy cloak also. And whosoever shall compel thee to go a mile, go with him twain. Give to him that asketh thee, and from him that would borrow of thee turn not thou away. Ye have heard that it hath been said, Thou shalt love thy neighbour, and hate thine enemy. But I say unto you,_

Love your enemies, bless them that curse you, do good to them that hate you, and pray for them which despitefully use you, and persecute you; That ye may be the children of your Father which is in heaven: for he maketh his sun to rise on the evil and on the good, and sendeth rain on the just and on the unjust. For if ye love them which love you, what reward have ye: do not even the publicans the same? And if you salute your brethren only, what do ye more than others: do not even the publicans so? Be ye therefore perfect, even as your Father which is in heaven is perfect."

In the above text, Jesus quotes certain recourses and rights that the people of God had under the laws of **The Old Testament**. According to **The Old Testament** (Exodus 21:24; Leviticus 24:20; Deuteronomy 19:21) if a man put out the eye of another man, the man who lost the eye had the legal right to put out the eye of the man who caused him harm.

"Eye for eye, tooth for tooth, hand for hand, foot for foot, Burning for burning, wound for wound, stripe for stripe." (Exodus 21: 24, 25)

The disciples and multitudes--in awe and amazement--listened to Jesus as He taught them on Mount Carmen to exemplify forgiveness, love and compassion by forsaking their own personal right for revenge and vengeance. Christ taught them to love their enemies. This concept at that present time was unknown and foreign to the Jewish mindset.

Jesus instructed the people on the mountainside to not fight back, but to turn the other cheek, *so to speak*, in a conscience effort to demonstrate to the offenders the love of

God. Jesus also taught His people to make a greater effort to illustrate His love by unselfish giving and by going another mile in demonstrating His patience and kindness. He said, *"And if any man will sue thee at the law, and take away thy coat, let him have thy cloak also. And whosoever shall compel thee to go a mile, go with him twain."*

During the time of Jesus, Rome had a Headquarters in Jerusalem for its military. It was the right of a Roman soldier to order and insist that a Jewish person or non-Roman citizen help him carry his equipment for at least one mile beyond the gates of Jeruselem as the soldier moved about on his military assignment. This greatly frustrated and irritated the Jews and probably gave the Roman soldier a great sense of superiority and satisfaction.

What Jesus was trying to do in instructing the people to not resist evil (fight back, murmur, complain) was to equip them to be conveyers of His message of the **"Power of Love"**. Jesus wanted the Jews to relay this message to the unbeliever which the prophet Jeremiah had passed on to their ancestors to lure them out of their rebellion and captivity *"...saying, Yea, I have loved thee with an everlasting love: therefore **with lovingkindness have I drawn thee.**"* (Jeremiah 31:3b)

Jesus taught: *"...Love your enemies, bless them that hate you, and pray for them which despitefully use you, and persecute you; That ye may be the children of your Father which is in heaven: for he maketh his sun to rise on the evil and on the good, and sendeth rain on the just and on the unjust"*

Saints and Sinners, God loves us *so much*!!!

In His **Sermon on the Mount** Jesus taught men to love one another...even their enemies...and leave the judgment and vengeance to God. If we would only follow this commandment, like Mahatma Gandhi, Reverend Dr. Martin Luther King Jr. and Jesus, we too could make a positive and lasting impact upon the world we live in.

"And great multitudes came unto him having with them those that were lame, blind, dumb, maimed, and many others, and cast them down at Jesus' feet; and he healed them: In so much that the multitude wondered, when they saw the dumb to speak, the maimed to be whole, the lame to walk, and the blind to see: and they glorified the God of Israel. Then Jesus called his disciples unto him, and said, I have compassion on the multitude, because they continue with me now three days, and have nothing to eat: and I will not send them away fasting, lest they faint in the way...And Jesus saith unto them, How many loaves have ye? And they said, Seven, and a few little fishes... And he took the seven loaves and the fishes, and gave thanks, and brake them, and gave to his disciples, and the disciples to the multitude. And they did all eat, and were filled..." (Matthew 15:30-32, 34, 36-37a)

In the above text, God's love through Christ moved him to compassion to heal and feed the infirmed and hungry masses of humanity yearning for fulfillment. And His love continues to reach-out to the empty, sick and impoverish today, to bless, empower and make them whole. **Our Lord is still in the blessing business! *HALLELUHAH!***

"Then one of them, which was a lawyer, asked him a question, tempting him, and saying, Master, which is the great commandment in the law? Jesus said unto him, Thou shalt love the Lord thy God with all thy heart, and with all thy soul, and with all thy mind. This is the first and great commandment. And the second is like unto it, Thou shalt love thy neighbour as thyself. On these two commandments hang all the law and the prophets." (Matthew 22:35-40)

A Pharisee lawyer asked our Lord, tempting him, a very profound and thought-provoking question in the above text. To paraphrase him, he asked, *"Master, which one of the commandments is the most important, greatest and preeminent one?"* Jesus did not question the attorney's motive but He answered the question: *"Thou shalt love the Lord thy God with all thy heart, and with all thy soul, and with all thy mind. This is the first and great commandment."*

Love is the greatest of all virtuous qualities. If we truly loved God as He loves us, we would cling to and obey His every command with joy and we would love and respect our neighbors and continuously seek their good…War and turmoil would cease and peace like a soft and delicate blanket would gently cover the land, as a mother her sleeping child, and heaven would come to eternally dwell on earth.

Unfortunately my earthly carnal friends, we cannot love God until we accept and allow the supernatural love of His Son Christ Jesus to be spread abroad in our hearts by the Holy Spirit. Only then, when this happens, will wars cease and peace, like a river, flood the world with gladness; and joy, unspeakable and full of glory bust from golden clouds and abundantly shower its' ecstatic treasures upon us. ***Hallelujah!***

"And he entered again into the synagogue; and there was a man there which had a withered hand. And they watched him, whether he would heal him on the Sabbath day; that they might accuse him. And he saith unto the man which had the withered hand, Stand forth. And he saith unto them, Is it lawful to do good on the Sabbath days, or to do evil? To save life, or to kill? But they held their peace. And when he had looked round about on them with anger, being grieved for the hardness of their hearts, he saith unto the man, Stretch forth thine hand. And he stretched it out: and his hand was restored whole as the other." (Mark 3:1-5)

Remember the Sabbath and keep it Holy. Saturday was a day of rest for the Jewish people. It was a day to honor God and reframe from works. When Jesus entered the synagogue on the Sabbath day, he encountered a man with a withered hand and the love of God in Him for humanity droved Him to take action and heal the man even on the sacred day of rest. But first, before He healed the man, Christ would ask the Pharisees and Sadducees (church folks) a question to prick their conscience and maybe stir up a sense of righteousness in them. *"Is it lawful to do good on the Sabbath days, or to do evil? To save life, or to kill?"* They said nothing. As a matter of fact they had no concern or desire for the man with the withered hand to be healed. They themselves were all right, and this was all that mattered to them. They were more concerned about the day of the week than about the sufferings of a fellow soul…this angered Christ. He wanted them to love and to care for one another just as His Heavenly Father *love* and *care*. But in spite of the people uncaring and hard hearts, and the lingering threat of the penalty of death that hovered over His head, Christ, the Son of God healed the man anyway. After all, that is why he came: *"The Spirit of the Lord is upon me, because he hath anointed me to preach the gospel to the poor; he hath sent me to heal the brokenhearted, to preach deliverance to the captives, and recovering of sight to the blind, to set at liberty them that are bruised, to preach the acceptable year of the Lord."* (Luke 4:18-19) John the Apostle said, *"For God so loved the world, that he gave his only begotten Son, that whosoever believeth in him should not perish, but have everlasting life. For God sent not his Son into the world to condemn the world; but that the world through him might be saved."* (John 3:16,17)

"Jesus went unto the mount of Olives. And early in the morning he came again into the temple, and all the people came unto him; and he sat down, and taught them. And the scribes and Pharisees brought unto him a woman taken in adultery; and when they had set her in the midst, They say unto him, Master, this woman was taken in adultery, in the very act. Now Moses in the law commanded us, that such should be stoned: but what sayest thou? This they said, tempting him, that they might have to accuse him. But Jesus stooped down, and with his finger wrote on the ground, as though he heard them not. So when they continued asking him, he lifted up himself, and said unto them, He that is without sin among you, let him first cast a stone at her. And again he stooped down, and wrote on the ground. And

they which heard it, being convicted by their own conscience, went out one by one, beginning at the eldest, even unto the last: and Jesus was left alone, and the woman standing in the midst. When Jesus had lifted up himself, and saw none but the woman, he said unto her, Woman, where are those thine accusers: hath no man condemned thee? She said, No man, Lord. And Jesus said unto her, Neither do I condemn thee: go, and sin no more." (John 8:1-11)

The wages of sin is death: *"And the man that committeth adultery with another man's wife, even he that committeth adultery with his neighbour's wife, the adulterer and the **adulteress** shall surely be put to death."* (Leviticus 20:10)

An adulteress sat before Jesus, in her shamefulness, naked and trembling and covering her head, bracing herself for the impact of the heavy rocks she envisioned would soon be coming her way to render her unconscious so death could carry off her sinful soul to deposit it in hell. She was scared, frightened…and *alone,* she thought. For a moment of pleasure, she had sinned against the very Lord whom she now shuddered before and she timidly watched him and waited as He knelt and wrote in the sand. She knew she was guilty…so she covered her head and waited for the stones.

What can wash away my sins? Nothing but the blood of Jesus. What can make me whole again? Nothing but the blood.

The stones never came………………

Her accusers silently wandered off to search their own heart and to think upon their own sins in silent, leaving the woman alone in the presence of Jesus. His warm eyes pardoned and embraced her as he admonished her to *"go and sin no more."*

What manner of love is this, that lets sinners go free?

What manner of love is this, which pardon wretches like you and me?

God sent His Only Begotten Son into the world to demonstrate to **man** His love for **us**. His desire is that no man perishes but that all men and women might come to repentance. As Christ hung on the cross between two thieves, and the people mocked him, He prayed to the Father, *"Father forgive them; for they know not what they do."* Our Lord Jesus Christ could have called legions of angels to come to His rescue but He would not because:

If He had spilled the *bitter cup of suffering* and come down from the cross, Life and eternal hope for man would have forever been spilled and lost.

It wasn't the nails in His hands and feet that held him to the tree.

It was the *Greatness of His Love* that caused Him to bleed and die for thee.

The Apostle Paul asked the question: *"Who shall separate us from the love of Christ? Shall tribulation, or distress, or persecution, or famine, or nakedness, or peril, or sword? As it is written, For thy sake we are killed all the day long; we are accounted as sheep for the slaughter. Nay, in all these things we are more than conquerors through him that loved us. For I am persuaded, that neither death, nor life, nor angels, nor* *principalities, nor powers, nor things present, nor things to come, Nor height, nor depth, nor any other creature, shall be able to separate us from **the love of God, which is in Christ Jesus our Lord**.*" (Romans 8:35-39)

Readers, may the love of God demonstrated through His Son Jesus, *manifest* itself in you and I; and like a match struck in kindling of the forest ignites in us a fire which burns and perpetually spreads within us and throughout the world... God, let not Your fiery love in us consume lukewarm and icy *hearts* but let Your fervent love *through us* passionately and eternally ignite aglow every cold and lukewarm *soul*, setting ablaze the whole globe with the shekinah warmth and glory of Your loving, adorable and serene presence. So let it be!

Amen! Amen!

THE FATHER'S LOVE
FOR HIS PRODIGAL SONS

"And he (Jesus) *said, A certain man had two sons: And the younger of them said to his father, Father, give me the portion of goods that falleth to me. And he divided unto them his living. And not many days after the younger son gathered all together, and took his journey into a far country, and there wasted his substance with riotous living. And when he had spent all, there arose a mighty famine in that land; and he began to be in want. And he went and joined himself to a citizen of that country; and he sent him into his fields to feed swine. And he would fain have filled his belly with the husks that the swine did eat: and no man gave unto him. And when he came to himself, he said, How many hired servants of my father's have bread enough, and to spare, and I perish with hunger! I will arise and go to my father, and will say unto him, Father, I have sinned against heaven, and before thee, And am no more worthy to be called thy son: make me as one of thy hired servants. And he arose, and came to his father, But when he was yet a great way off, his father saw him, and had compassion, and ran, and fell on his neck, and kissed him. And the son said unto him, Father, I have sinned against heaven, and in thy sight, and am no more worthy to be called thy son. But the father said to his servants, Bring forth the best robe, and put it on him; and put a ring on his hand, and shoes on his feet: And bring hither the fatted calf, and kill it; and*

let us eat, and be merry: For this my son was dead, and is alive
again; he was lost, and is found. And they began to be merry.
Now his elder son was in the field: and as he came and drew
nigh to the house, he heard musick and dancing. And he called
one of the servants, and asked what these things meant. And he
said unto him, Thy brother is come; and thy father hath killed
the fatted calf, because he hath received him safe and sound. And
he was angry, and would not go in: therefore came his father out,
and entreated him. And he answering said to his father, Lo, these
many years do I serve thee, neither transgressed I at any time thy
commandment: and yet thou never gavest me a kid, that I might
make merry with my friends: But as soon as this thy son was
come, which hath devoured thy living with harlots, thou hast
killed for him the fatted calf. And he said unto him, Son, thou
art ever with me, and all that I have is thine. It was meet that we
should make merry, and be glad: for this thy brother was dead,
and is alive again; and was lost, and is found." (Luke 15:11-32)

In the parable recorded above, Jesus tells a story of a
father and his two sons. One of the sons, the younger one, is
openly rebellious, unfaithful and undisciplined. He demands
his inheritance from his father and he goes into the bright
lights of the big city and squanders the money on wine,
women and riotous living. The eldest son, on the other hand,
is on the surface disciplined and obedient. He faithfully stays
at home and works his father's fields but within his heart
perfect love has waxed cold.

Before **He told** the parable in Luke chapter 15, verses
11 through 32 which theologians throughout the centuries

have dubbed **the parable of the Prodigal Son,** Jesus told two other parables. One of a precious coin lost in the house and another of a stranded and lost sheep. I, through personal revelation, have come to the conclusion that these three parables are meant to be told *together* as Christ told them. Instead of being three separate parables, I would like to relate them as being three chapters of the same novel, with different plots but a central theme to relate a particular and specific message. Therefore, by the grace of God and the guidance of His Spirit, I have linked the three parables together as one in this chapter I've adequately entitled, **"The Father's Love for His Prodigal Sons."**

In these three parable, Jesus shows the love of his Father and God's compassion for lost souls in a portrait of a young woman who loses a coin from her wedding dowry; in the snapshot of a shepherd who loses a sheep from his fold; and in the disguise of a doting father who loses his youngest son to the satanic streets of the **far-away country of sin** and who consoles and ministers to his disillusioned eldest son who bear anger and contempt for the younger brother who has volitionally, through riotous living, squandered a hefty portion of the family income.

Let's read how Jesus began these three parables. *"Then drew near unto him all the publicans and sinners for to hear him.* **_And the Pharisees and scribes murmured, saying, This man receiveth sinners, and eateth with them_**. *And he spake this parable unto them, saying, What man of you, having an hundred sheep, if he lose one of them, doth not leave the* *ninety and nine in the wilderness, and go after that which is lost, until he find it? And when he hath found it, he layeth it on his shoulders rejoicing. And when he cometh home, he calleth together his friends and neighbors, saying unto them, Rejoice with me; for I have found my sheep which was lost. I say unto you, that like wise joy shall be in heaven over one sinner that repenteth, more than over ninety and nine just persons, which need no repentance."* (Luke 15:1-7)

I would like to submit to you that this parable in Luke 15:4-7 about the lost sheep *also represents* and *is symbolic* of the parable of the younger son, whom we as church folks refer to as the **prodigal son.** The Oxford American Dictionary refers to **prodigal** as: *a recklessly extravagant person or a recklessly wasteful person.* When, we as church folks refer to prodigal, we're usually talking about a *backslider* whom has left the church or forsaken his biblical principles.

In Luke's recording of the parable of the lost sheep, a Shepherd has one hundred sheep under his care and protection. Most of them are grazing in the grass, filled and satisfied. But there is one younger sheep that is not. Daily this sheep had been daydreaming; he had been gazing into the horizon and wondering about the green grass and foliage that beckoned in the distant valley. How *fascinating, exciting* and *enjoyable*, he imagined it would be if he ventured forth to partake-of and explore this new horizon. And he did…and found himself lost just like the younger son we will elaborate on from the text whereby we began this chapter of the book:

Luke chapter 15, verses 12 through 24 records the story of a young man who approaches his father and demands his inheritance. He's bored with the daily monotonous and rigorous activities of working on the farm and he has heard about the big city, and about the girls and about the parties...and he just can't wait any longer to explore and enjoy this forbidden world. He boldly goes before his father and demands his money. He wants it and he wants it now. The wise old man did not argue with the young lad. He divided amongst his two boys the money that they would have eventually inherited at his demised.

The youngest son took his money, packed his belongings on the wagon and hitched it to his donkey and excitedly, with anticipation of a new life, went up the road that led from his father's house towards the bright lights of the big city that lie many many miles away.

The naïve young man, upon entering the city, was immediately surrounded by prostitutes, pimps, dope dealers and hustlers. He found himself in a place and among people where he did not fit. He was honest but his associates were not. He shared his drugs and liquor but they did not. He gave and they took.

With his large bankroll, he was the host of the party. He bought and spent and spent and bought until soon all of his money was gone.But that was not the worst of it. As soon as his money was gone, his friends were gone and a famine came to the land. The young man had good work ethics but jobs and food were hard to find in such a devastated and depressed economy.

After selling his ring, his donkey and some of the clothes off his back to make ends meet, he found himself in deeper poverty. Eventually he got a job feeding hogs, but the pay was not enough for him to properly eat so he found himself longing for the slop he fed the swine.

At home, many miles away, the father sat on his front porch looking afar off down the road, praying and waiting patiently for his youngest son to come home...but there was no sign of him. Day-in and day-out and night after night, the father kept praying for the return of his son. His prayers reached heaven and the Holy Spirit tugged on the young man's heart. *"Come now, and let us reason together, saith the Lord: though your sins be as scarlet, they shall be as white as snow; though they be red like crimson, they shall be as wool."* (Isaiah 1:18)

The tugging shook the young man to consciousness and he came to himself and said, *"...How many hired servants of my father's have bread enough and to spare, and I perish with hunger! I will arise and go to my father, and will say unto him, Father, I have sinned against heaven, and before thee, And am no more worthy to be called thy son: make me as one of thy hired servants."* (Luke 15:17b-19)

The younger son began his long journey home guided by the prayers of the loving father...prayers of love sent with arms of mercy and grace to embrace and lead the young man safely home.

One bright sunny day, the father sat on his porch looking down the road. In the great distance he saw a speck appear. He kept looking as the speck enlarged and became what he imagined was a figure of a man afar off. As the figure came closer, he noticed the gait and the familiar swing of the arms. The arms did not swing as high and the feet did not project the lively mannerism or agility of his son's usual walk but... IT WAS HIS SON!

The old man jumped off the porch and like an Olympian Champion ran down the road. The servants watched, thinking him mad, but he did not notice them. He could only see the deflated and sad countenance of his son as they approached one another. When he reached his son, the father felt upon his son's neck, lavishing his dirty face with kisses.

The son repented, but before the son could ask to be one of his father's hired servants and live in the servant quarters, the father said to his servants, "...*Bring forth the best robe, and put it on him; and put a ring on his hand, and shoes on his feet: And bring hither the fatted calf, and kill it; and let us eat, and be merry: For this my son was dead, and is alive again; he was lost, and is found. And they began to be merry.*"

In the parable of the lost sheep, the lost sheep was found and the angels in Heaven threw a party rejoicing at the sheep's return. Now the son was home and the father and his servants rejoiced with music and dancing and the best of foods celebrating the return of a son that"...*was dead and is alive again; he was lost, and is found...*"

The prodigal son and the lost sheep both strayed away from home and became lost in unfamiliar surroundings, but the searching prayers of both the shepherd and the father went looking to find and return them home. When the tasks were accomplished and the sheep and son were both back safely under the protection of their guardians, both the father and shepherd rejoiced and sanctioned a party to celebrate the homecomings. So is it with God. At the return of the lost sheep, Luke recorded these words of Christ, *"I say unto you, that likewise joy shall be in heaven over one sinner that repenteth, more than over ninety and nine just persons, which need no repentance."*

Looking at the glad countenance of their Lord's face, when a lost sheep or backslider returns to Christ or a wretched sinner come to Him for salvation, the angels explodes with joy and all of heaven celebrates.

Just as the lost sheep and the younger son stories are similar, I believe the stories of the lost coin in the house and the eldest brother are symbolically the same story. They both remain at home in the house but they become distant and unavailable to their owners. Jesus tells the parable of the lost coin in these words: *"Either what woman having ten pieces of silver, if she lose one piece, doth not light a candle, and sweep the house, and seek diligently till she find it? And when she hath found it, she calleth her friends and her neighbours together, saying, Rejoice with me; for I have found the piece which I had lost. Likewise, I say unto you, there is joy in the presence of the angels of God over one sinner that repenteth."* (Luke 15:8-10)

At the time the younger son returned home, the eldest son was working hard in the field under the heat of the blazing sun but night soon approached and his workday came to an abrupt end. He was tired. As he approached the house, he heard sounds of joy. There were music and dancing and carousing. "What could this great celebration be?", he thought. When he met a servant in the yard he asked and the servant told him of his brother's return and the elation and joy upon his father's face upon his brother's return. This news should have made the elder brother happy but it did not. The warm love in his heart for his younger brother had grown cold.

I wrote in my book **The Power of Love** these words concerning the elder brother: "*In the book of Luke, chapter 15, when the prodigal son returned home, there was joy in heaven. The father was happy and even the angels danced a jig. But the brother who had stayed home all of this time and who had toiled in the noonday sun, was upset and angry. Seemingly, he had a right to be upset. The father was throwing a party for this wayward brother of his who had disgraced the family. The father had never surprised him with a party and surely, he had been faithful."* I go on to say in the book, "*So often, people in the church are like the elder brother who stayed at home when it comes to forgiveness and acceptance of backsliders and sinners. At times, we are self-righteous and only look at the sins that are most obvious. While we are focusing on **the lust of the flesh; the sins of the lust of the eyes** and **the pride of life** are consuming us.*"
I end my commentary on the elder brother with these words,

"The brother who stayed at home needed grace too. He didn't realize it, but he did. He was saturated with the sin of pride and he lusted in his heart for the affection and attention his younger brother was receiving from the father.

Beneath the outer layer of his sanctification—anger, bitterness and hatred stirred. Even though he had stayed home with the father all these years; he did not know the heart of the father. Yes, he had worked in the father's field and he had slept in the father's bed, and ate at the father's table, but he did not have good fellowship or an intimate relationship with the father. If he had known the father intimately, he would have known that the father also wanted him to party and enjoy life. The father loved him also. And at any time he could have given himself a party. He had the resources. After all, all the father had belonged to him."

The elder brother became angry at the news that his father had killed the fatted calf for the younger brother and was throwing the younger brother a party. The elder brother sulked and would not go in the house to celebrate with his friends and his family. Realizing this, the loving father came out to him and reassured him of his love for him and the father patiently and gently reminded his elder son that everything in the father's possession was there also for his pleasure and enjoyment and that he too were free and welcome at anytime to throw himself a party.

In the parable of the prodigal sons, the father went outside searching until he found his eldest son, just as the woman with the lost coin searched the house until she had found it.

Using the term **prodigal** as we do in the twenty-first century Church referring to those in backslidden conditions, I would like to suggest that both of the man's sons were prodigals. One, like the coin, was lost in the house and the other like the sheep ventured away from the flock into a strange and far country to become lost.

But by the grace of God, the love of the father for both boys was equal--determined and unparalleled. I believe, the father's words, prayers and love for his two sons would eventually reach the cords of their hearts and draw them both into the **Great House** to feast with God and His servants, the angels, at the great wedding feast of the Lamb! **Hallelujah!**

If you're unsaved and reading this book, it is God's love and goodness that has drawn you to this encounter with the reality and truth of His love for you...and to His desire and will for you to have eternal life. Repent of your sins and ask God today to forgive you and to save you. He will.

God loves you and He's waiting with outstretched arms for you to come.

"And this is the will of him that sent me, that every one which seeth the Son, and believeth on him, may have everlasting life: and I will raise him up at the last day." (John 6:40)

"Verily, verily, I say unto you, He that heareth my word, and believeth on him that sent me, hath everlasting life, and shall not come into condemnation; but is passed from death unto life." (John 5:24)

Romans 10:13 reads: *"For whosoever shall call upon the name of the Lord shall be saved."*

Let's call upon the Lord now, by saying this prayer: *"God, I've sinned against heaven and against You and I have done this evil in Your sight. Please forgive me of all my sins and cleanse me from all unrighteousness. Accept me into Your Kingdom and teach me how to walk in this earth and to live a life that is pleasing and acceptable in Your sight. I confess with my mouth that Jesus is Lord and I believe in my heart that God raised Him from the dead. Thank you Lord for saving me and lead me to a Church that teaches the sincere milk and meet of Your word so that I may grow thereby. As I daily seek You through Your word and in prayer, reveal Yourself more and more unto me through Your **manifest presence** and **by faith**. I thank you God for saving me and granting me eternal life. In Jesus Name. Amen."*

If you have prayed this prayer with Godly sorrow and conviction, the God who love you so much that He gave His only Begotten Son has heard you and saved you and the angels in Heaven are joyfully celebrating your entry into the sheepfold of the Great Shepherd (Psalm 23), our Lord and Savior Jesus Christ. *Congratulations* and *welcome* into the **Kingdom of God**!

THE LOVE CHAPTER

"Though I speak with the tongues of men and of angels, and have not charity, I am become as sounding brass, or a tinkling cymbal. And though I have the gift of prophecy, and understand all mysteries, and all knowledge; and though I have all faith, so that I could remove mountains, and have not charity, I am nothing. And though I bestow all my goods to feed the poor, and though I give my body to be burned, and have not charity, it profiteth me nothing. Charity suffereth long, and is kind; charity envieth not; charity vaunteth not itself, is not puffed up, Doth not behave itself unseemly, seeketh not her own, is not easily provoked, thinketh no evil; Rejoiceth not in iniquity, but rejoiceth in the truth; Beareth all things, believeth all things, hopeth all things, endureth all things. Charity never faileth: but whether there be prophecies, they shall fail; whether there be tongues, they shall cease; whether there be knowledge, it shall vanish away. For we know in part, and we prophesy in part. But when that which is perfect is come, then that which is in part shall be done away. When I was a child, I spake as a child, I understood as a child, I thought as a child: but when I became a man, I put away childish things. For now we see through a glass, darkly; but then face to face: now I know in part; but then shall I know even as also I am known. And now abideth faith, hope, charity, these three: but the greatest of these is charity." (I Corinthians 13:1-13)

The Greek language has several words for love but in this chapter I will define three of those Greek words but I will focus on only one. One of the Greek words I will define is **philao. Philao** means brotherly love or love between friends. From the Greek word philao, we get the word for one of our most famous cities in America, **Philadelphia.** Philadelphia therefore is dubbed the **City of Brotherly Love**.

Another Greek word used for love is **eros**. A word we get from this term is **erotic**. So **eros** is *erotic or sexual love* between a man and a woman.

The third Greek term used for love is **agape**. This is the word used in the 13th chapter of First Corinthians and the word we will focus on. Agape is dubbed "**the God kind of love**". *Agape love* is *unselfish*. It is *unconditional love*. With **agape** you can love someone when he or she doesn't love you back.

I quoted from the KJV when recording the 13th chapter of I Corinthians and the term the KJV use for **love** is **charity**. Please do not let this confuse you.

In the twelfth chapter of **I Corinthians** Paul speaks of the gifts of the Spirit that Christ has given to the Church. He ends this chapter by exhorting us to "*...covet earnestly the best gifts:*" and then he says: "*and yet shew I unto you a more excellent way.*"

The more excellent way Paul is speaking of is the receiving, developing and exercising of the supernatural agape love of God. Agape love is a spiritual fruit that can only be birthed and shed abroad in our hearts by the Holy

Ghost. **Man** cannot exemplify or manifest this kind of love on his own.

Let's examine this supernatural and spectacular love recorded in the 13ᵗʰ chapter of **I Corinthians**. Paul begins like this: *"Though I speak with the tongues of men and of angels, and have not charity, I am become as sounding brass, or a tinkling symbal."* To paraphrase Paul, he enlightened the Corinthians that if he spoke every known lanquage in the world and could even speak in the tongue of angels and did not have agape love, he was just making noise or talking gibberish. He goes on to say in verse 2 that if he had the gift of prophecy, and understood all mysteries and all knowledge; and had the kind of faith to speak to mountains and watch them move aside and did not love unselfishly, unconditionally and with veracity, his many gifts profited him nothing.

In verse 3 Paul speaks of great sacrifices. He says, *"And though I bestow all my goods to feed the poor, and though I give my body to be burned, and have not charity, it profiteth me nothing."* **Paul!** You mean that if a person gives away all his money to feed hungry and starving people and allows himself to be put on a stake and burned alive for a great and notable cause that that person's sacrifice would be in vain if it is not done in love? **Paul!** How could one make such sacrifices and not have love? Could one do these things only to be seen or to be applauded? Could one sacrifice one's life for some misguided principle or selfish motive? *"Yes"* Paul confirms; without love, *"...it profited...nothing."*

Love is long suffering, Paul says, and is kind. It does not envy others, or puff and vaunt up itself with pride. Love does not behave in an unseemly way and love is not selfish. Love is not easily offended or irritated and love sees and thinks the best, even when men sees and thinks the worst. Love does not rejoice when men fall into sin or at sinful acts but love rejoices only when Truth triumphs and prevails. Love upholds all things, believeth all things, hopeth all things, and endureth all thing. *"Love"*, Paul understood, *"never fails."*

One day, in eternity's future, there will be no need for the gift of prophecy or the word of knowledge. These gifts will pass away. Even now, when we are operating in the supernatural gift of the word of knowledge, we see and know so little. And with the gift of prophecy, we can only speak so little. *"For we know in part, and we prophesy in part"*, Paul informed us.

But one day, when the love of God is perfected in us and we're in our glorified bodies, we'll have no need for supernatural gifts for we'll dwell and operate in the supernatural love of God.

We are required and we must; however, mature in love while we dwell in this flesh. As a matter of fact, God's love should spread and grow in the hearts of believers. And like Paul, we should grow in understanding and mature from selfish childish deeds and thinking to unselfish and mature acts of compassion and love. We must grow –up and put away childish things.

At the present, we cannot see spiritual things as clearly as we desire to, but one day, *heavenly things* will be clearly revealed to us. The darkened glass will turn crystal clear and we'll see the glory of God and things in their proper perspective and in all their total beauty as we enjoy eternity with Christ our Lord, the heavenly angels, our saved love ones, and our neighbors and friends.

In Eternity, our souls will experience immeasurable peace and joy and shall be opened to unlimited wisdom and knowledge and we'll have no need for earthly spiritual gifts.

But there are things that we experience in this presence world that are unchangeable and eternal and will never pass away, such as: **Faith**, **Hope** *and* the greatest of all never-ending virtues--Love ....**God is Love**.

May God bless the readers of this book and instill and shower upon each and every one of you the awareness of the immeasurable comfort and security of His love. I pray that you know and experience the depth of the sacrifice Christ made to purchase your freedom when He hung, bled and died on a wooden cross and that you'll come to love Him because of the simple and undeniable fact that He first loved you.

May the love of God continuously rest, rule and abide *in* and *upon* us throughout all Eternity.

Amen.

~

CHAPTER 3

~

WHAT I BELIEVE

(Basic Belief Requirements for a Christian)

(*B*UT SANCTIFY THE *Lord God in your hearts: and be ready always to give an answer to every man that asketh you a reason of the hope that is in you with meekness and fear:*) I Peter 3:15

If asked, many in America would say that we live in a *new age of enlightenment* and in a *global world society*...A world and age whereby **many souls** are seeking their own paths to the eternal and abundant life and there's no longer a need for the Judeo Christian Bible as the moral road map to chart the way to heaven and glory. *"There's many ways to God"*, the New Agers of today proudly preach and proclaim. But the Bible teaches that: *"There is a way which seemeth right unto a man, but the end thereof are the ways of death."* (Proverbs 14:12)

If the wise man King Solomon was here today, he would remind us: "*The thing that hath been, it is that which shall be; and that which is done is that which shall be done: and **there is no new thing under the sun**.*" (Ecclesiastes 1:9)

If Solomon were here with us in 2018, he would warn us through personal experience and through tears that there's nothing new under the sun. What men are doing today to erect their own pathways to joy, self-sufficiency, happiness and heaven has already been tried.

Solomon being the wisest and richest man in the Old Testament experienced everything in life that influence, power and money could buy in his search to obtain fulfillment, satisfaction, and enlightenment, only to discover in the end, that all was *vanity, vanity and vexation of spirit.*

In his golden years, after having experimented with everything he could in life to obtain pleasure; including a vast collection of mansions, women, and treasures, the wise old preacher Solomon came to the conclusion as he ended his Ecclesiastical sermon, "*Let us hear the conclusion of the whole matter: **Fear God, and keep his commandments**: for this is the whole duty of man. For God shall bring every work unto judgment, with every secret thing, whether it be good, or whether it be evil.*" (Ecclesiastes 12:13, 14)

We live in a day of great technology. The world is changing by the second before our very eyes as the nations of the world, through speedy transportation and the internet, come together, as one-world-society, like the people did in the Eleventh chapter of **Genesis**, to share their knowledge, wisdom and assets in a single effort to make for *themselves* a name and to build a tower to heaven without the approval, assistance, direction and help of God.

*"And the Lord came down to see the city and the tower, which the children of men builded. And the Lord said, Behold, the people is one, and they have all one language; and this they begin to do: and now nothing will be **restrained** from them, which they have imagined to do."* (Genesis 11: 5, 6)

Man, because of his *sinful* and *unstable* heart, need restraint for: *"The heart* (of man) *is deceitful above all things, and desperately wicked: who can know it?"* (Jeremiah 17:9)

If present-day **man** with his evil heart is allowed by God to do all that advanced technology and today's scientific discoveries afford him, mankind will self-annihilate. As in the days of the tower of Babel, God's grace and love still must intervene to restrain **man** in order to keep him from hell and from his many inventive and creative ways of self-destruction.

In our churches today, there are many preachers who claim to be believers of Christ who are teaching a universal type doctrine, insisting in their messages that ***there are many ways to God***. Muslims, Buddhists, Hindus, Jehovah Witnesses, Scientologists and many other religious organizations that Christian once believed to be false sects are now gradually being accepted by the Church as being legitimate religions.

The Holy Bible teaches us that there is only one name given among men whereby we must be saved and that name is Jesus. And there is only one Book to guide us and that book is the Bible (The Word of God).

The things that the Bible calls and labels as sin, we must also accept as being sinful.

Homosexuality is a sin...unfortunately same sex-marriages are being ordained, sanctioned and legitimized by preachers, agenda-oriented judges and politicians as being acceptable and normal acts when God through His Word brands homosexuality an abomination...even nature agrees with God and silently rebels and screams out against it.

One of our most notable politician, the first black president of the United States, confesses that he is a Christian, yet he is for *legalized-abortion* and for homosexual couples having some of the same rights that has only, until this present time in the U.S.A, been granted to married couples. **This should not be.** Christians should honor God's word and should love and cherish the things that God loves *and reject and despise* the *t*hings that God hates.

Since Believers of Christ are commanded to pray for their leaders and those that are in authority, we as saints of God should bombard the heavens with prayer for our presidents and our nation.

God, observing from heaven, must be weeping rivers of tears as He watches American doctors daily shedding, shredding and spilling the innocent flesh and blood of human infants...casting little corpses into the garbage to be disposed of as *dung* or *filthy rags.* Just as God judged Sodom and Gomorrah for their immorality and sin, America *must* and *will* be judged.

The reason the Holy Spirit has led me to write this book is to: **laud the Bible as God's inspired Word and as being the only source to true salvation; alert God's people to the false new-age teachings that are creeping into the Church;** and **to warn and deter true-seekers of God from going down the wrong path**.

In order for one to be saved and avoid the torments of hell, he or she must believe that Jesus is the Son of God; and that Christ was born of a virgin; and that he died on a cross and three days later rose from the dead so that whosoever believeth in Him should not perish but have everlasting life.

Peter admonished us to *"…be ready always to give an answer to every man that asketh us a reason of the hope that is in us with meekness and fear."* This book, I have suitably entitled; **What I Believe,** is designed to equip us as believers of Christ with Truth so that we as children of God will be prepared to readily answer this crucial question the Apostle Peter so eloquently posed to us concerning our belief; with reverence, integrity and sound conviction.

Paul admonished his young disciple, Timotheus, with these words: *"Study to show thyself approved unto God, a workman that needeth not to be ashamed* (confused, humiliated or reluctant), *rightly dividing the word of truth."* (II Timothy 2:15)

Believers of Christ and *seekers of God*, we must know the truth and know what we believe if we are to ascend the right stairway to the True and Living God of Heaven. In this book, I will guide you through scriptures and instruct you on what the Bible and Our Lord and Savior Jesus Christ profess about the way to heaven…Christ spoke of only one pathway to the Celestial City and <u>it was</u>, <u>is</u> and <u>always will be</u> *a strait and narrow* one.

In 1983 when I accepted my call to the ministry, I wanted to be sure that God was really *speaking to* and *calling* me so I did something that I would not advise others to do, especially those mature in the faith. I held my bible in my hands and I asked God to reassure me that he was calling me and to lead me to scriptures in the **Holy Writ** that would further advise me; and verify my calling. I opened the Bible and my eyes felt upon scriptures that I was not currently familiar with…I opened the book and my sight felled upon II Timothy, the fourth chapter. It read: *"I charge thee therefore before God, and the Lord Jesus Christ, who shall judge the quick and the dead at his appearing and his kingdom: Preach the word; be instant in season, out of season; reprove, rebuke, exhort with all longsuffering and doctrine. For the time will come when they; will not endure sound doctrine; but after their own lusts shall they heap to themselves teachers, having itching ears; And they; shall turn away their ears from the truth, and shall be turned unto fables. But watch thou in all things, endure afflictions, do the work of an evangelist, make full proof of thy ministry."* (II Timothy, chapter 4:1-5)

Those Rhema words from Second Timothy, chapter four became my calling card. As I read those words I knew I was being sent as an evangelist to declare and preach the infallible Word of God.

God forewarn us in **II Timothy** the fourth chapter *that a time would come* when men would not preach the true and infallible Word of God but they would preach what the world and their congregations wanted to hear...*That time has come* and is presently here. That's why as a true Evangelist of the Cross, I must write this book to proclaim like the saints of old, that Jesus is Lord and that there is no other name among men given whereby we must be saved. I must proclaim to the world **What I Believe**.

Let's Pray: Heavenly Father, use this book to inspire, motivate, equip and enlighten your blood bought church and cause them to proclaim to those who lie in spiritual darkness the truth that Jesus is Lord and that there is no other way to **YOU** but through your Beloved Son.

Father God, Give me what to say as I write this book, which You have assigned and ordained for me to write, even before the foundation of the world...Anoint me to hear Your voice. Continue to forgive me and cleanse me from all my sins, known and unknown and give me a burden and a heart to warn the lost and hurting masses that are on the *broad road* to hell and destruction that You are the **Way**, the **Truth** and the **Light**.

Father, those whom you have called, draw by Your Holy Spirit; save them and shed Your love abroad in their hearts. **In Jesus' Name!**

We're forever love, worship; and give You the praise and glory.

Your friend and Evangelist,
Robert L. Shepherd Jr.

A CHRISTIAN MUST BELIEVE IN THE INERRANCY OF THE BIBLE

In order to be a Christian, one must believe in the inerrancy of the Bible and extol the Bible as the infallible word of God.

Many today, such as the successful and infamous writer, Dan Brown, do not believe in the truths recorded in the Bible. Dan Brown books and *movies of his writings* have indoctrinated and enlightened millions in the world to his stance and beliefs that our Lord Jesus Christ was only a fallible, pathetic *mere* mortal; when in reality, Jesus Christ *was* and *eternally is* **The Sinless SON of GOD.**

Just like Dan Brown, a number of biblical scholars and preachers today do not take the **Lord Jesus Chris**t and the **Bible** seriously and do not believe that the Bible is the Logos word of God. But whether one believes that the Bible is the inspired Word of God or not, does not change the fact that the contents of the Bible have been proven, by men, to be accurate, through thousands of years of scrutiny and use. Every since God gave Moses the Ten Commandments and he Torah, men have tried to live up to the precepts and laws of God's instruction to the human race. Faithful and devout men and women have, to the best of their abilities, endeavored to walk in moral excellence, and live lives of integrity, obedience and holiness, as God, through His word, would have them.

Timothy recorded: *"All scripture is given by the inspiration of God, and is profitable for doctrine, for reproof, for correction, for instruction in righteousness: That the man of God may be perfect, thoroughly furnished unto all good works."* (II Timothy 3:16, 17)

The Apostle Peter wrote: *"Knowing this first, that no prophecy of the scripture is of any private interpretation. For the prophecy came not in old time by the will of man: but holy men of God spake as they were moved by the Holy Ghost."* (II Peter 1:20, 21)

Prophets, kings and *holy men*, during the period of **The Old Testament,** recorded on scrolls what God inspired and instructed them to put into print and there were always the voices of *devout obedient servants* to relay to God's people His word. However, from the book of Malachi until **The New Testament** period, God prophetic voice was silent. Nevertheless, His chosen people had His recorded Word to encourage them and give them hope.

In the New Testament, after the Son of God had come upon the scene and willingly given His life for man's redemption and returned to glory, God sent the Holy Spirit into the world to lead and guide His Apostolic Church unto **all Truth.**

The Holy Ghost, now being in the earth, would inspire chosen **Men of God** once again to record HIS WORD in order to *lead, teach* and *guide* His blood-bought Church unto maturity and holiness and to keep them in the world; *from the* **Evil One.**

After the Apostle John recorded the book of Revelation *given* to him by our Lord and Savior Jesus Christ on the Island of Patmos, the Bible *became complete* in its text and contents. Throughout the years, the increase of knowledge, the advancement in technology and new scientific discoveries, have *confirmed* to studious observers the prophecies in the Bible to be mind-boggling; and have *verified* the Bible's historical and scientific accuracy to be astronomically phenomenal in its veracity. When examined closely, new archeological evidence and findings *are consistently proving* the Bible *correct* in its recorded historical facts and events; and in its depiction of *people, places* and things of the past.

Without fail, as new evidence come to light; *confirmed claims* and *fulfilled prophecies* of the Bible are recognized and appreciated by **Believers** as *signs* and *factual proof* of the Bible's authenticity.

No other manuscript *of antiquity* has been proven to be as correct and accurate in its contents as the recorded information in the Bible is. Daily, as time advances and man's knowledge increases, the documented mass of *unsubstantiated data* in the Bible *is steadily being* substantiated and proven *as* **fact**. Only the hand of an **Omniscient Divine Creator** could have given us such a supernatural and magnificent book whose number of *preserved copies* vastly outnumbers in quantity every other known *single literary work* of antiquity.

Whether one believes the Bible to be the word of God or not, does not change the fact that God's word will not *go out and come back void*. What God has supernaturally recorded through the pen of about forty men over a period of 1500 years in 66 books and recorded and preserved on hundreds of antique scrolls; HE will *surely* watch over and bring to pass. Everything thing that **God** said HE will do in His Word, He will definitely do. **Scripture**, **time** and **truth** have taught us that: God nurtures, protects and *"watches over His Word to perform it."*

Heaven and earth shall one-day pass away—*melt with a fervent heat*—but God's Word shall remain forever. One day, there will be a new heaven and a new earth for *presently*, *gradually* and *suddenly*; the current heaven and earth is fading and passing away: **transforming and transitioning into** *a new state of being*.

But even though the present heaven and earth is *passing away* and is being revised and renewed, be assured and know that God's **Word** will never change...God's Word has been eternally established.

Throughout its history, men have tried to rid the world of the **Word of God**. The Bible has been burned, banned and discarded in an attempt to wipe it from off the face of the earth, yet the Bible today is the number one *best seller* in the world and there are, at any present moment, more bibles on the face of the earth than any other book.

The prophet Amos spoke of there one-day being a famine; and the famine would not be for *bread and water* but it would be *for the word of God*. After the apostolic church-age and the fall of the Roman Empire, there came a dark period in the world whereby the word of God was not readily available and accessible to the common man.

Throughout the middle age, the Catholic Church (headed by the Pope), held the Bible tightly in its grasp; and the Holy Text was only for the priesthood, the educated; the rich and the elite: Those who were trained and versed in Hebrew, Latin, Aramaic or Greek.

Early biblical translators, educators, writers and *proponents* such as William Tyndale, John Wycliffe, John Milton, John Bunyan, Martin Luther and *many* others, were either imprisoned, banished, persecuted, beheaded or burned at the stake for their unshakeable stance for the Bible. These men, enduring personal risks and sacrifices, endorsed and fought for the *accessibility* and *distribution* of the Word of God to the common man in the common man's own language.

On the continent of Europe, when men and women protested and rebelled against the teachings of the Pope and the Catholic Church, many of them were martyred for their Faith; and for their position that *every man* should have access to the Bible and should be able to worship God as they saw fit. These **protestors** were called **Protestants**.

In the early 1600's, biblical scholars were assigned and authorized by King James (The King of Great Britain, France and Ireland) to translate the Bible into the English language so that every citizen of the English Kingdom could have access to the biblical text. Thus, in 1611 the **Authorized King James Version** appeared upon the world scene and it *has been in print* every since, along with numerous of other Bible Interpretations and Bible Translations.

The "**Apocrypha**" is the name given to a collection of Jewish books, or portions of books, mostly written during the closing centuries of the BC Era and in the dawning years of the AD epoch.

Many earlier bibles, some which included the **apocrypha writings**, *did not include* it as being a part of canon or being inspired of God; but they inserted the **apocrypha writings** in the middle or back of the Bible, as historical information and as *reference material*.

However, the Protestant Church does not consider these books as being the inspired Word of God. The Apocrypha books are outlandish in many of its claims; and a great deal of the *statements and assertions* in this literature has been proven *to be* untrustworthy and false.

Some of the apocrypha books are considered *as the* **Word of God** by the Catholic Church and are included in the Catholic Bible…but the Protestants reject all of the Apocrypha Texts and do not include them or accept them as the **Inspired Word of God.**

The Hebrew people were the *chosen people* of God and they were given the awesome task of truthfully recording and preserving God's Word. In the Hebrew Bible, which is divided into three sections, (the **Law** [Torah], **The Psalms** and **The Prophets),** the *Apocrypha books do not appear.* Even until this day, the *Apocrypha writings* are not a part of the Hebrew canon.

Sometime, between the third century B.C. and the dawning of the A.D. era, the **Septuagint**, a Greek translation of the Hebrew Bible, was produced in Alexandria, Egypt. In the **Septuagint**, A group of seventy scribes and translators added *apocrypha writings* by unsanctioned Jewish authors, as being part of the biblical text.

Today's Protestant Churches only accept the 39 books of the **Old Testament** recorded in the Hebrew Canon and the 27 books of the **New Testament,** as being God's inspired Word…and rightly so.

The 27 books of the **New Testament** are lauded and extol by both the Catholic and Protestant Church as being the inspired Word of God. Therefore, neither Protestant nor Catholic believers accept other literature *written* during the *early church period* (such as the **Gospel of Thomas** and the **Epistle of Barnabas**) as being a part of **New Testament canon** *or* as being the **Inspired Word of God**.

Some educated skeptics (knowing that there are old Mesopotamian stories of antiquity, Greek mythologies and others ancient global stories of creation and of God, which they consider to be similar to the Hebrew canon and predate the Bible) conclude that the Hebrews stole many of their ideas and concepts of God and creation from other ancient people and texts.

This idea is as far-fetched and ridiculous as the global ancient myths of ancient civilizations and is as baseless and foolish as the superstitious and stagnating ideas of modern day ancient tribesmen who are presently living naked or scantily clad, deep within the inhumane jungles of the world, worshipping ancient idol gods (demons) to their own hurt;

and are (in a technological advanced modern world) existing like primitive savages.

The God of the Hebrews is a God of wisdom, progress and order and HE would not and did not permit His people to commit human sacrifices or require them to perform foolish feats *in order* to please Him. However, the **God of Creation** did require obedience, faithfulness, righteousness and the *sacrificial shedding of the blood of animals* for the remission of sin.

Now, finally and once and for all times, this requirement has been *eternally* met and achieved by Jesus Christ, the Son of God, when He willingly came to the earth and shed His own precious blood for the propitiation of man's sin and *for our redemption*. (In a coming chapter of this book, I will discuss the **shedding of blood** in more details).

Like, I pointed out at the beginning of this chapter: In order to be a Christian, one must believe that the Bible is the infallible Word of God and one must follow and obey its laws and precepts. Unfortunately, many today have discarded the Bible and now deem it as just another ancient text, when in fact, the Bible is God's **instruction manual** or **road map** to an abundant life here on earth and an eternal one in the impending New Heaven and Earth.

My prayer is that the Spirit of God has inspired me to say something in this chapter *and in the following ones*, that will prick your heart and stir up your faith to believe in God and in His Holy Word...But most of all, I pray that the Holy Spirit will draw you unto God and woo you unto accepting Jesus Christ as your Lord and Savior.

IN ORDER TO BE A CHRISTIAN ONE MUST BELIEVE IN GOD: THE TRIUNE CREATOR AND REDEEMER

In order to be a Christian, one must believe that God is a **Divine Eternal Triune Being** who with unlimited wisdom, knowledge and power *created* the heaven and the earth and man in His own image.

*"In the beginning **God** created the heaven and the earth. And the earth was without form, and void; and darkness was upon the face of the deep. And the **spirit** of God moved upon the face of the waters. And God **said**..."* (Genesis 1:1-3a)

*"In the beginning was the **Word**, and the **Word** was with God, and the **Word** was God. The same was in the beginning with God. All things were made by **him**; and without **him** was not any thing made that was made...And the **Word** was made flesh, and dwelt among us, (and we beheld **his** glory, the glory as of **the only begotten** of the Father,) full of grace and truth."* (John 1:1-3, 14)

In verses one through three of Genesis, Moses, in his writings, reveals God, the Creator, as a Triune Being (**The Holy Trinity**). Let's put on our spiritual scuba gear and dive into the waters of Holy Writ to observe **God** in His **Tri-unity**. Like in the children's game **Finding Waldo**, let's look into the venire of God's word with our spiritual binoculars and find *every name*, *every presence* and *every mention* of God. In verse one of Genesis, when Moses says, *"In the beginning **God**..."*, he's speaking of **God the Father**. When Moses goes on to say in verse two, *"...And the **spirit of God** moved upon the face of the waters"* he's speaking of the **Holy Ghost** or the **Holy Spirit**.

Finally, in verse 3, when Moses records, *"And **God said**..."* he is, by divine revelation from the Spirit of God, *making reference* to the **Word** or the **Logos**, also known as **Jesus Christ; the Son of God**.

John literally began his gospel, by proclaiming Jesus as the **Word** of God in his portrayal of Christ role in the creation of heaven and earth. John says: *"In the beginning was the **Word**, and the **Word** was with God, and the **Word** was God. The same was in the beginning with God. **All things were made by him; and without him was not any thing made that was made.**"*

The **Word** was with **God** in the beginning and the **Spirit** was with **God** in the beginning, because the **Word** and the **Spirit** *was* and *is* **God**. In other word, **God**, the **Holy Spirit** and the **Word** are *ONE*. God is a **Triune Being** and the **Creator** of all things.

Charles Darwin believed and propagated a theoretical gospel that man evolved from a *single cell creature* to eventually, over billions of years, become a monkey which would in due course derive into a man. Darwin gospel is called the **Law of Evolution**. The Law of Evolution is a theoretical law, which eliminates God from the creation process. This law proclaims that there is no God but only *evolutionary processes* whereby only **Chance** *matters* and whereby only the strongest of creatures survive in a chaotic and unpredictable universe.

According to the Law of Evolution, God did not create the heaven and the earth, or the physical universe. All things, according to the Law of Evolution, derived from a random **big bang**, or atomic explosion in the heavenlies; whereby the stars and planets and all other universal entities would eventually (over billions and billions or years) come into existence. But in the word of God given to Moses (**Genesis**), we are told that God created the heaven and the earth and all the individual creatures in them, by the *power of His word* and by the *Omniscience of His will*. Then God created man in His own image and gave him dominion over the physical earth. Let's read Moses recording of man's creation from the book of Genesis. *"And God said, __Let us make man in our image__, after __our likeness__: and let them have dominion over the fish of the sea, and over the fowl of the air, and over the cattle, and over all the earth, and over every creeping thing that creepeth upon the earth. So God created man in his own image, in the image of God created he him; male and female created he them."* (Genesis 1:26-28)

When God said, *"Let us make man in our image"*, **who was He speaking too?** I'll tell you…God was speaking to Himself. God, as a Triune Being, was speaking to **Himself**, the **Son** and the **Holy Spirit**.

"And The LORD GOD formed man of the dust of the ground, and breathed into his nostrils the breath of life; and man became a living soul." (Genesis 2:7)

In order to be a Christian, one must believe in God: the Triune Creator and that all things were made by Him and without Him was not anything made that was made.

Did all creation began with a *random* Big Bang or is the bible right? Did God create heaven and earth and man in His own image?

To be an Atheist, one must have a very elevated and high degree of faith to believe that man derived from monkeys and that the universe, one day, without God's assistance, exploded into existence...and over billions of years developed into its present form. It does not take the unfathomable faith of an Atheist *to believe* that an **Eternal**, **Wise**, **Omnipotent**, **Omniscient FIRST CAUSE** spoke and *ordered* the universe into being.

To believe a Devine God created the heaven and the earth only takes a measure of faith...And God has instilled a measure of faith into the heart and bosom of every human being He created.

"*In the beginning*" Moses said, "*God created the heaven and the earth.*" Later, Moses records, "*And God created man in his own image...*"

To be an atheist, one must muster up enough faith to believe in *the impossible, the implausible* and *the improbable;* but to be a Christian, one only need a *measure of faith* to trust and believe that a All-knowing, Caring and Wise God created the universe and created man; in **HIS** own image.

In order to be a Christian, one must believe that there is a Caring, Good and Wise God, but one must also believe that there is an Evil and Deceitful Devil. Jesus confronted this creature *a number of occasions* when He walked the earth as a man, and our Lord left us record of *this being* and *this creature's* intent and goal for **Man**. Jesus said, *"The thief (Devil) cometh not, but for to steal, and to kill, and to destroy: I am come that they might have life, and that they might have it more abundantly."* (John 10:10)

Reader, if you are not a believer, I pray that what I have written in this chapter has pricked your *measure of faith* and aroused hope in you--and has inspired you to believe that; **In order to be a Christian, one must believe in God: The Triune Creator and Redeemer.**

CHRISTIANS MUST BELIEVE IN THE VIRGIN BIRTH

In order to be a Christian, one must believe in the virgin birth: that a woman without sexual intercourse, or the semen of a man, supernaturally, through the overshadowing of the Holy Spirit, gave birth to a son...our Lord and Savior Christ Jesus.

Many in the church today, even some preachers behind the pulpit, do not believe in the virgin birth of Christ; but yet they are calling themselves Christians. This is a paradox and an oxymoron. One cannot be a Christian without believing in the virgin birth of the Son of God.

In the seventh chapter of the **Book of Isaiah**; the nations Syria, Ephraim, and the son of Remaliah, came together to destroy Judah, whose King at the time was Ahaz.

They conspired among themselves: "*Let us go up against Judah and vex it, and let us make a breach therein for us, and set a king in the midst of it, even the son of Tabeal.*" (Isaiah 7:6) God overheard these nations in their plot and conspiracy against His people and God responded: "*Thus saith the Lord God, It shall not stand, neither shall it come to pass...Moreover the Lord spake again unto Ahaz, saying, Ask thee a sign of the Lord thy God; ask it either in the depth, or in the height above. But Ahaz said, I will not ask, neither will I tempt the Lord. And he said, Hear ye now O house of David; Is it a small thing for you to weary men, but will ye weary my God also? Therefore the Lord himself shall give you a sign; Behold, a virgin shall conceive, and bear a son, and shall call his name Immanuel."* (Isaiah 7:7, 10-14)

God sent his prophet Isaiah to inform Ahaz, the **King of Judah**, of the futility of the plot against him and the nation of Judah. Isaiah, through the instruction of God, then requested King Ahaz to ask for a sign or a miracle; for a confirmation and assurance that *God had truly spoken* and would stop the takeover plot and spoil the enemy's plan. Ahaz responded, "*I will not ask, neither will I tempt the Lord*". Isaiah, now a little irritated and annoyed by the King's response and lack of faith said, "*Hear ye now O house of David; Is it a small thing for you to weary men, but will ye weary my God also?*"

We weary God and try God's patience when we refuse to obey Him. God wants us to come to him for answers.

James said in the fourth chapter of his epistle that *we have not because we ask not.* If you are perplexed and confused and need an answer, go to God in prayer: *Ask and it shall be given unto you, seek and you shall find, knock and the door shall be opened unto you.* God is pleased at those who trust and seek him and He rewards those who diligently seek him.

When God requested Ahaz to ask Him for a sign and Ahaz refused to ask for a sign, Isaiah proclaimed that the Lord Himself would give the King and the nation of Judah a sign. "*Behold*", Isaiah said, "*a virgin shall conceive, and shall bear a son, and shall call his name Immanuel.*"

It is probably best for us that King Ahaz did not ask for a sign to confirm the promises of God. Ahaz, being mortal like us, probably would have asked for an immediate miracle to verify the words of God's prophet.

God had given him a choice to ask for any miracle—one of his choosing. But he refused to ask God for a sign. In Ahaz small mind, asking God for a sign would be *tantamount* to testing God or akin to doubt. And because Ahaz refused to ask the Almighty for a sign, God Himself gave one of the greatest prophesy and sign in all of Scripture. God foretold of a miraculous feat of a virgin conceiving and birthing a son without sexual intimacy; who would bear the name of Immanuel. **Immanuel means God with us**.

Through His Son Jesus, God would come down from heaven and tabernacle among us. God, through His Son Jesus, would enter the earth and walk, talk, eat and fellowship with men. And eventually, He would die on a cross so that we might have eternal life.

Isaiah also prophesied in chapter 10 of his book; in verses six and seven, *"For unto us a child is born, unto us a son is given: and the government shall be upon his shoulder: and his name shall be called Wonderful, Counselor, The mighty God, The everlasting Father, The Prince of Peace. Of the increase of his government and peace there shall be no end, upon the throne of David, and upon his kingdom, to order it, and to establish it with judgment and with justice from henceforth even for ever. The zeal of the LORD of hosts will perform this."*

In the above text, the prophet Isaiah said that *a child would be born for us*, and *a son would be given for us*. This was confirmed in the New Testament by Jesus Himself when He told Nicodemus, *"For God so loved the world, that he gave his only begotten Son, that whosoever believeth in him would not perish, but have everlasting life."* (John 3:16)

In the New Testament, all of the gospel writers except Mark and John *literally gives* detail accounts of the virgin birth of Christ. Matthew records this," *Now the birth of Jesus Christ was on this wise: When as his mother Mary was espoused to Joseph, before they came together, she was found with child of the Holy Ghost. Then Joseph, her husband, being a just man, and not willing to make her a publick example, was minded to put her away privily. But while he thought on these things, behold, the angel of the Lord appeared unto him in a dream, saying, Joseph, thou son of David, fear not to take unto thee Mary thy wife: for that which is conceived in her is of the Holy Ghost. And she shall bring forth a son, and thou shalt call his name JESUS: for he shall save his people from their sins. Now all this was done, that it might be fulfilled which was spoken of the Lord by the prophet, saying, Behold, a virgin shall be with child, and shall bring forth a son, and they shall call his name Emmanuel, which being interpreted is, God with us. Then Joseph being raised from sleep did as the angel of the Lord had bidden him, and took unto him his wife:*

And knew her not till she had brought forth her firstborn son: and he called his name Jesus." (Matthew 1:18-25)

When Matthew recorded the words that, Mary espoused husband, Joseph *"knew her not"* his intent was to inform us that Joseph did not have sexual contact with his fiancé until after the birth of the Messiah...that the birth of Christ was a supernatural act of God.

At the time of the birth of our Lord and Savior Jesus Christ, Herod was the appointed king of the region. Matthew records: *"When Herod the king had heard these things, he was troubled, and all Jerusalem with him. And when he had gathered all the chief priests and scribes of the people together, he demanded of them where Christ should be born. And they said unto him, In Bethlehem of Judaea: for thus it is written by the prophet, And thou Bethlehem, in the land of Judah, art not the least among the princes of Judah: for out of thee shall come a Governor, that shall rule my people Israel."* (Matthew 2:3-6)

The scribes and Pharisees knew through prophecy that Christ would be born in Bethlehem of Judah so Matthew in the above text recorded it.

Luke speaks of the virgin birth in these words, *"And in the sixth month the angel Gabriel was sent from God unto a city of Galilee, named Nazareth, To a virgin espoused to a man whose name was Joseph, of the house of David; and the virgin's name was Mary. And the angel came in into her, and said, Hail, thou that art highly favoured, the Lord is with thee: blessed art thou among women. And when she saw him, she was troubled at his saying, and cast in her mind what manner of salutation this should be. And the angel said unto her, Fear not, Mary: for thou hast found flavor with God. And, behold, thou shalt conceive in thy womb, and bring forth a son, and shalt call his name JESUS. He shall be great, and shall be called the Son of the Highest: and the Lord God shall give unto him the throne of his father David: And he shall reign over the house of Jacob forever: and of his kingdom there shall be no end. Then said Mary unto the angel, How shall this be, seeing I know not a man? And the angel answered and said unto her, The Holy Ghost shall come upon thee, and the power of the Highest shall overshadow thee: therefore also that holy thing which shall be born of thee shall be called the Son of God."* (Luke 1:26-35)

Old Testament prophecies speak of a coming Messiah, and the New Testament verifies and confirms the coming of the Son of God into the earth. A virgin did conceive and bare a Son and He gave His life so that men could return to the Creator and the God of all flesh.

God so loved the world that He disrobed His Son of His Heavenly glory and don upon Him an earth suit, sensitive to decay, pain and even death so that He could dwell among us and be touched by the feelings of our infirmities and sympathize with our plight. He came as a man to teach us how we could live the abundant life and walk in the dominion He gave Adam (the original man) before Adam sinned against Him.

Like Christ, God wants to save men and fill them with His Spirit so that they can walk, talk and operate with the mind of Christ. Philippians chapter two admonishes us to *"Let this mind be in you, which was also in Christ Jesus: Who, being in the form of God, thought it not robbery to be equal with*

God: But made himself of no reputation, and took upon him the form of a servant, and was made in the likeness of men: And being found in fashion as a man, he humbled himself, and became obedient unto death, even the death of the cross. Wherefore God also hath highly exalted him, and given him a name which is above every name: That at the name of Jesus every knee should bow, or things in heaven, and things in earth, and things under the earth; And that every tongue should confess that Jesus Christ is Lord, to the glory of God the Father." (Philippians 2:5-11)

In order to be a Christian, one must believe, literally, that our Lord and Savior Christ Jesus took upon himself *the form of a man* and died for the sin of men. The virgin birth of Christ was an actual event in the history of man and it is not only recorded and reference to in the bible, but also in secular historical accounts. I hope and pray that this chapter of the book "**WIB**" has fertilized your heart to accept and believe in the virgin birth of Christ. For there is no other option: **In order to be a Christian, one must believe in the virgin birth of Christ.**

CHRISTIANS MUST BELIEVE IN CHRIST'S CRUCIFIXION AND RESURRECTION FROM THE DEAD

In order to be a Christian, one must believe in the crucifixion and bodily resurrection of Christ from the grave—that Christ suffered and died a brutal and agonizing death on the cross and that on the third day rose victorious from the dead *in order* that those who would believe on (in) Him would also one day arise from spiritual and physical death unto everlasting life.

A Christian must believe that the Son of God willingly and purposefully left His throne in Heaven and came to the earth to physically suffer and die for the *sin of mankind,* which *originated* with the fall of Adam and Eve in the garden of Eden.

At the moment Adam and Eve hearkened to the lies of the devil, they inadvertently became *willing victims,* captured by **Evil** and imprisoned by <u>sin</u> and **death**. The heart of God was broken and grieved by Adam and Eve's betrayal, but yet He was not caught off guard or surprised. God, being Omniscient, fore-knew that **man** would rebel against Him and listen to the false-assuring-seductive lies of the **Deceitful One**...God knew in advance that Adam and Eve, misled by the devil into believing that they could become *more-wise* and **more-God-*like*,** would disobey Him and willingly partake of the forbidden fruit…but **The Almighty** was not bewildered. God, in His omniscience, knew **man** would fall from his earthly throne and lose his power and control of the world to Satan…but HE was prepared.

God had the **SOLUTION**…

The Father of Lies lied to Adam and Eve…The duo did not become more God-like; they became more like the devil when they received within themselves the *Knowledge of Evil* and the *nature of sin*. **Sin**, in its *very intrinsic nature* is the mother (author) of death. Therefore, when Adam and Eve sinned they died spiritually—thus permitting the **soul** (their invisible **logic** *eye* to the physical environment) to *take control* of their corporal existence and haphazardly lead and guide them in the earth without the leadership of their God-breathed **spirit-man** which, *now*, being separated from the **SPIRIT of God**, was dead; lying *in-dominantly* within them… Before Adam and Eve sinned, their **spirit man** was *connected* to the **Spirit of God** and **it** covered, ruled and led their soul and flesh in *holiness* and they were in tuned with their Creator God and *sinless*. Existing (*in pure light*), un-severed from **God's Spirit,** their spirit man enabled them (their souls) to walk, talk and exhibit God's Righteousness.

But, the instant Adam and Eve sinned they became lost and their spiritual eyes were darkened and sin reigned in them and through them and was genetically passed on to their children and to every boy and girl that would subsequently enter the earth.

God is Holy and He hates sin and sin cannot intimately come in contact with Him. Therefore God had to send His Son into the earth as a man to become **sin** for us...Thus, the Son of God was born into the earth, took upon Himself the cross and was crucified for **man's** sin in order to *reconcile* **man** back to his **CREATOR**.

Our Lord and Savior Jesus Christ willingly left His throne in Glory to suffer an agonizing and painful death on the cross so that we could be saved. **The price Christ paid was great**...but **Love** propelled Him. In Romans chapter eight the Apostle Paul proclaimed, *"He that spared not his own Son, but delivered him up for us all, how shall he not with him also freely give us all things?...For I am persuaded, that neither death, nor life, nor angels, nor principalities, nor powers, nor things present, nor things to come, Nor height, nor depth, nor any other creature, shall be able to separate us from the love of God, which is in Christ Jesus our Lord."* Roman 8:32-39)

Love propelled our Lord and Savior, Christ Jesus, to endure death and separation from His Father so that repentant souls could come back to God by renouncing their sins and proclaiming Jesus Christ as *Savior and Lord*.

The story in the Old Testament of Jonah being in the belly of a whale 3 days and 3 nights was *prophetic symbolism* of the Son of God's *three-day and night* stay in the heart of the earth. Christ, the Son of God, said, *"...An evil and adulterous generation seeketh after a sign; and there shall no sign be given to it, but the sign of the prophet Jonas: For as Jonas was three days and three nights in the whale's belly; so shall the Son of man be three days and three nights in the heart of the earth."* (Matthew 12:39, 40) All Christian **must** believe in the death and resurrection of the Lord Jesus Christ. The Messiah Himself prophesied His death and crucifixion in these words: *"And as Moses lifted up the serpent in the wilderness, even so must the Son of man be lifted up: That whosoever believeth in him should not perish, but have eternal life."* (John 3:14, 15)

It is recorded in the book of Numbers, chapter 21, that God's people sinned against Him by murmuring and complaining and by speaking against Moses, their God-chosen leader. They acted in doubt and unbelief when they said to Moses, *"...Wherefore have ye brought us up out of Egypt to die in the wilderness? For there is no bread, neither is there any water; and our soul loatheth this light bread."* (Numbers 21:5)

Because of their disdain and distrust in God and His ordained leadership, God judged them, and He sent serpents (poisonous snakes) into the camp to destroy them. The people of Israel had sinned...and the wages of sin was (and still is) death. Every man, woman, boy and girl that was bit by a serpent was infested by the poison of sin and in a *matter of time*...would die.

"Therefore the people came to Moses, and said, We have sinned, for we have spoken against the Lord, and against thee; pray unto the Lord, that he take away the serpents from us..." (Numbers 21:7)

Observing their penitent hearts, God informed Moses to make a brazen serpent, put it upon a pole and lift it up so that the whole camp *could* see it. Moses obeyed. *"...and it came to pass, that if a serpent had bitten any man, when he beheld the serpent of brass, he lived."* (Numbers 21: 9)

In John chapter 3, verses 14 and 15, Jesus spoke of this incident when He predicted that if He would be **lifted up from the earth** (crucified on a cross) He, like the brass serpent, would be the means whereby sinful men and women, having been poisoned by the inherited-sin-infested blood of Adam, could by choice, behold Christ the Messiah (**look up!**) and live.

The most seriously and critically ill patients, in Numbers chapter 21, which had been stung by the poisonous vipers, would be carried by their friends or loved ones in pain and agony to a spot in the camp where they could see the brazen serpent suspended on the pole. As they would glance up, with dimmed eyes affected by the poison rushing through their bodies, they would see the serpent (*which was a foreshadow of the crucified Christ*) and their health would be restored... They would live.

Others who were bitten, and were less delirious and less feeble than those carried to view the brazen image, would, on their own accord, look to the brazen serpent mounted-high atop the pole and *they too* would live. But some in disbelief refused to hear the prophet Moses and refused to believe that such a simple act of glancing upon a serpent on a pole could cease the effect of the deadly venom. These men and women, by their inactiveness and unbelief, would die by the sin-infested sting of the fiery serpents.

Today, in order to be a Christian, one must, through the gospel, symbolically come to the cross and observe the bloody figure of the Son of God hanging there, and believe that Christ literally died for his or her sins. Faith and salvation come only by hearing the word of God--the gospel (Good News) of Christ. When one hears it, just as in the wilderness when Moses instructed those bitten by the poisonous serpents to look upon the brass image suspended upon the pole in order to live--one must look to Christ and believe that He died for his or her sins and *only* in Christ is there salvation and *life abundant.*

My friend, don't fear Him...Submit all to Christ and trust Him. He will never leave or forsake us when our faith is stretched out, like a bridge, and suspended wholly upon Him–relying only upon the power of His precious blood, which He so willingly shed, to keep us from falling into the eternal **Lake of fire** which lies below. Every man, woman, boy and girl that come to God must cross this bridge of faith, *leaning, hoping* and *depending* on the finished work of Christ...and on Christ alone.

Throughout the bible, scripture foretells of Christ's death and crucifixion. The first mention in scripture of Christ's death and suffering takes place in the book of Geneses--after man's fall and spiritual separation from God. God addressed the devil in Genesis chapter 3 and verse fifteen with these words *"And I will put enmity between thee and the woman, and between thy seed and her seed: it shall bruise thy head, and thou shalt bruise his heel"*.

In the above passage, after Adam and Eve disobeyed God and ate of the forbidden fruit, God pronounced a curse on them and He also addressed the devil and foretold of his defeat and destruction. God told the serpent that He would put enmity between the seed of the woman and the serpent. And that the seed of the woman would deliver the serpent a fatal blow by bruising his head rendering him helpless; and by recovering the power and authority in the earth that Adam had surrendered to the serpent when Adam and Eve sin against God. When God spoke of the seed of the woman obtaining a bruise heel in His crushing of the serpent's head it was a prophesy of Christ death and suffering on the cross and of the precious blood Christ would shed on Calvary for our sin.

Christ death and suffering on the cross, made it possible for mankind to return to God. It gave us access once again to God and abolished the enmity that sin had placed between God and man. When Christ rose from the dead, after being crucified, He took His precious blood back to Heaven and placed it on the mercy seat before the present of His Father abolishing the enmity between God and those who would believe in Christ and His finished work at the cross. Only through crucifixion and the shedding of blood could Christ restore us back unto Himself and unto God. Jesus was inhumanely beaten and marred more than any man and His blood was spilled so that we could have life and life more abundantly. When Christ suffered and died for us on the cross, He fulfilled the prophesy in Genesis that predicted the heel of the seed of the woman would be bruise, when He, with His Mighty foot, would crush the head of the serpent.

God comparing Jesus horrific death and suffering on the cross to a bruised heel--a minor ailment, is beyond comprehension. Christ suffering and crucifixion was atrocious and horrendous, yet God compared it to a partially bruised foot. Maybe God could do this because He viewed His Son's victory on the cross as a feat that out weight Christ suffering. In God sight, Christ's victory made His suffering minuscule (something minor). The word of God in Hebrews 12: 8 says that Jesus "...*for the joy that was set before him endured the cross, despising the shame...*" Jesus looked beyond the cross and saw multitudes of souls that would come into the Kingdom because of His great sacrifice and this gave Him joy and the will and strength to endure the cross.

It was mandatory for Christ to come into the earth and die on a cross in order for Him to destroy the serpent and take back the authority in the earth, which the devil had deceived and bereft Adam of. And He *came willingly.*

Another chapter in the Old Testament that speaks of Christ's death and suffering is Psalms 22. Verse One of Psalms 22 prophesize what our Lord and Savior Jesus Christ would one day cry out as He hung from the cross: "**My God, my God, why hast thou forsaken me?** *Why art thou so far from helping me, and from the words of my roaring:*"

Other thoughts that would bombard and vex our Savior's mind as He hung on the cross were these: "*Our fathers trusted in thee: they trusted, and thou didst deliver them. They cried unto thee, and were delivered: they trusted in thee, and were not confounded. But I am a worm, and no man, a reproach to men, and despised of the people. All they that see me laugh me to scorn: they shoot out the lip, they shake the head, saying, He trusted on the Lord that he would deliver him: let him deliver him, seeing he delighted in him."* (Psalms 22: 4-8)

In verse sixteen through eighteen of Psalm 22, the word of God foretells of Christ crucifixion in these words: *"For dogs have compassed me: the assembly of the wicked have enclosed me: they pierced my hands and my feet. I may tell all my bones* (none of my bones shall be broken): *they look and stare upon me. They part my garments among them, and cast lots upon my vesture."*

Isaiah foretells of Christ suffering in chapter fifty and verse six with these words, *"I gave my back to the smiters, and my cheeks to them that plucked off the hair: I hid not my face from shame and spitting."* Isaiah chapter 53 verses 4-10 reads: *"Surely he hath borne our griefs, and carried our sorrows: yet we did esteem him stricken, smitten of God, and afflicted. But he was wounded for our transgressions, he was bruised for our iniquities: the chastisement of our peace was upon him; and with his stripes we are healed. All we like sheep have gone astray; we have turned everyone to his own way; and the Lord hath laid on him the iniquity of us all. He was oppressed, and he was afflicted, yet he opened not his mouth: he is brought as a lamb to the slaughter, and as a sheep before her shearers is dumb, so he openeth not his mouth. He was taken from prison and from judgment: and who shall declare his generation? For he was cut off out of the land of the living: for the transgression of my people was he stricken. And he made his grave with the wicked, and with the rich in his death; because he had done no violence. Neither was any deceit in his mouth. Yet it pleased the Lord to bruise him; he hath put him to grief: when thou shalt make his soul an offering for sin, he shall see his seed, he shall prolong his days, and the pleasure of the Lord shall prosper in his hand."*

The emphasis of this chapter in my book, "**What I Believe**", is to admonish the Church and the world that in order to be a Christian, one must believe in the physical death (crucifixion) and resurrection of Christ. Christ death and resurrection is *what make it possible* for men and women who believe in Him to have eternal life. If Christ did not die and *rise up* from the grave, our **faith,** as Christians, is in vain. One must not only believe that Christ died on the cross, one must also believe that Christ rose from the dead.

"But if there be no resurrection of the dead," Paul admonished and encouraged the Corinthian Christian, *"then is Christ not risen: And if Christ be not risen then is our preaching vain, and your faith is also vain. Yea, and we are found false witnesses of God' because we have testified of God that he raised up Christ: Whom he raised not up, if so be that the dead rise not. For if the dead rise not, then is not Christ raised: And if Christ be not raised, your faith is vain; ye are yet in your sins. Then they also which are fallen asleep in Christ are perished. If in this life only we have hope in Christ, we are of all men most miserable."* (I Corinthians 15:12-17)

Acts 4:12 lets us know that there is no other name given under heaven whereby one can be saved but the name of our Lord and Savior Jesus Christ. This is *good news* and the only *good news* pertaining to life after death. Paul puts it this way in **I Corinthians** chapter 15, verses one through eight: *"Moreover, brethren, I declare unto you the* **gospel** *which I preached unto you, which also ye have received, and wherein ye stand; By which also ye are saved, if ye keep in memory what I preached unto you, unless ye have believed in vain. For I delivered unto you first of all that which I also received, how that* <u>**Christ died for our sins**</u> *according to the scriptures; And* <u>**that he was buried, and that he rose again the third day**</u> *according to the scriptures: And that he was seen of Cephas, then of the twelve: After that, he was seen of above five hundred brethren at once: of whom the greater part remain unto this present, but some are fallen asleep. After that, he was seen of James; then of all the apostles. And last of all he was seen of me also, as of one born out of due time."* When Paul wrote this letter to the Corinthian church he stated in the text above that many of the people whom had literally seen Jesus after his crucifixion and resurrection were still alive...they were living eyewitnesses to Christ's resurrection who could verify Paul's story.

In this part of the book, I will be what it might seem to some as redundant or repetitious as I give the accounts of the four gospel writers of the crucifixion and resurrection of Christ. All four of the gospel writers give a vivid account of Christ crucifixion and resurrection. For chronology sake, I will give these accounts in the order scripture record them;

starting with Matthew. In Matthew chapter 27, scriptures state that *"When the morning was come, all the chief priests and elders of the people took counsel against Jesus to put him to death: And when they had bound him, they led him away, and delivered him to Pontius Pilate the governor."* (Matthew 27:1-2)

When the governor of Judea, Pontius Pilate, examined Christ, he found Him innocent and desired greatly to release him, but the Jewish leadership would not have it...they wanted Christ dead.

Eventually, Pontius Pilate, (even after warning from His wife not to consent to the death of Christ) gave in to the Jews request. *"Then the soldiers of the governor took Jesus into the common hall, and gathered unto him the whole band of soldiers. And they stripped him, and put on him a scarlet robe. And when they had plaited a crown of thorns, they put it upon his head, and a reed in his right hand: and they bowed the knee before him, and mocked him, saying, Hail, King of the Jews! And they spit upon him, and took the reed, and smote him on the head. And after that they had mocked him, they took the robe off from him, and put his own raiment on him, and led him away to crucify him...And when they were come unto a place called Golgotha, that is to say, a place of a skull, They gave him vinegar to drink mingled with gall: and when he had tasted thereof, he would not drink. And they crucified him, and parted his garments, casting lots: that it might be fulfilled which was spoken by the prophet, They parted my garments among them, and upon my vesture did they cast lots...Then were there two thieves crucified with him, one on the right hand, and another on the left. And they that passed by reviled him, wagging their heads, And saying, Thou that destroyest the temple, and buildest it in three days, save thyself. If thou be the Son of God, come down from the cross... And about the ninth hour Jesus cried with a loud voice, saying. Eli, Eli, lamasabachthani? That is to say My God, my God, why hast thou forsaken me?...And straightway one of them ran, and took a sponge, and filled it with vinegar, and put it on a reed, and gave him to drink...Jesus, when he had cried again with a loud voice, yielded up the ghost.*" (Matthew 27:27-31, 33-35, 38-40, 46, 48, 50) Matthew goes on to say, "*When the even was come, there came a rich man of Arimathaea, named Joseph, who also himself was Jesus' disciple: He went to Pilate, and begged the body of Jesus. Then Pilate commanded the body to be delivered. And when Joseph had taken the body, he wrapped it in a clean linen cloth, and laid it in his own new tomb, which he had hewn out in the rock: and he rolled a great stone to the door of the sepulcher, and departed...In the end of the Sabbath, as it began to dawn toward the first day of the week, came Mary Magdalene and the other Mary to see the sepulcher. And, behold, there was a great earthquake: for the angel of the Lord Descended from heaven, and came and rolled back the stone from the door, and sat upon it. His countenance was like lightning, and his raiment white as snow: And for fear of him the keepers did shake, and became as dead men. And the angel answered and said unto the women, Fear not ye: for I know that ye seek Jesus, which was crucified. He is not here: **for he is risen**, as he said, Come, see the place where the Lord lay:*" (Matthew 27:57-60, Matthew 28:1-6)

Mark, in his gospel, records Jesus crucifixion and resurrection in these words. "And they bring him unto the place Golgotha, which is, being interpreted, the place of a skull. And they gave him to drink, wine, mingled with myrrh: but he received it not. And when they had crucified him, they parted his garments, casting lots upon them, what every man should take. And it was the third hour, and they crucified him. And the superscription of his accusation was written over, THE KING OF THE JEWS. And with him they crucify two thieves; the one on his right hand, and the other on his left. And the scripture was fulfilled, which saith, and he was numbered with the transgressors...And Jesus cried with a loud voice, and gave up the ghost. And the veil of the temple was rent in twain from the top to the bottom. And when the centurion which stood over against him, saw that he so cried out, and gave up the ghost, he said, "Truly, this man was the Son of God." (Mark 15:22-28, 37-39)

Mark conveys Christ resurrection from the dead with the following words: *And when the Sabbath was past, Mary Magdalene, and Mary the mother of James, and Salome, had bought sweet spices, that they might come and anoint him (Christ Jesus). And very early in the morning the first day of the week, they came unto the sepulcher at the rising of the sun. And they said among themselves, Who shall roll us away the stone from the door of the sepulcher? And when they looked, they saw that the stone was rolled away: for it way very great. And entering into the sepulcher, they saw a young man sitting on the right side, clothed in a long white garment; and they were affrighted. And he saith unto them, Be not affrighted: Ye seek Jesus of Nazareth, which was crucified:* **_he is risen_**; *he is not here: behold the place where they laid him."* (Mark 16:1-6)

Luke records our Lord and Savior Jesus Christ crucifixion and death with these words: *"And there were also two other, malefactors, led with him to be put to death. And when they were come to the place, which is called Calvary, there they crucified him, and the malefactors, one on the right hand, and the other on the left. Then said Jesus, Father, forgive them; for they know not what they do. And they parted his raiment, and cast lots. And the people stood beholding. And the rulers also with them derided him, saying, He saved others; let him save himself, if he be Christ, the chosen of God. And the soldiers also mocked him, coming to him, and offering him vinegar, and saying, If thou be the king of the Jews, save thyself. And a superscription also was written over him in letters of Greek, and Latin, and Hebrew, THIS IS THE KING OF THE JEWS...And it was about the sixth hour, and there was a darkness over all the earth unto the ninth hour. And the sun was darkened, and the veil of the temple was rent in the midst. And when Jesus had cried with a loud voice, hesaid, Father, into thy hands I commend my spirit: and having said thus, he gave up the ghost"* (Luke 23:32-38, Luke 23:44-46))

Luke records the resurrection thus wise: *"Now upon the first day of the week, very early in the morning, they came unto the sepulcher, bringing the spices which they had prepared, and certain others with them. And they found the stone rolled away from the sepulcher. And they entered in, and found not the* body of the Lord Jesus. And it came to pass, as they were much perplexed there-about, behold, two men stood by them in shining garments: And as they were afraid, and bowed down their faces to the earth, they said unto them, "Why seek ye the living among the dead"? **He is not here, but is risen**: remember how he spake unto you when he was yet in Galilee, Saying, The Son of man must be delivered into the hands of sinful men, and be crucified, and the third day rise again. And they remembered his words, And returned from the sepulcher, and told all these things unto the eleven, and to all the rest." (Luke 24:1-9)

Christ's disciple and Apostle John recorded these words concerning Christ crucifixion: "And he bearing his cross went forth into a place called the place of a skull, which is called in the Hebrew Golgotha: where **they crucified him**, and two other with him, on either side one, and Jesus in the midst."

Of Christ's resurrection John records: "Mary Magdalene came and told the disciples that she had seen the Lord, and that he had spoken these things unto her. Then the same day at evening, being the first day of the week, when the doors were shut where the disciples were assembled for fear of the Jews, came Jesus and stood in the midst, and saith unto them, Peace be unto you. And when he had so said, he shewed unto them his hands and his side. Then were the disciples glad, when they saw the Lord." (Matthew 20:18-20)

Each of the four gospel writers gives a different aspect of the crucifixion and resurrection of Christ from different points of view, focusing on different facets of the incidents but their facts can all be collaborated when viewing them as a whole. For instance, there were two angels on the scene of Christ's resurrection. Luke focuses on both angels, but Mark focuses only on one. Whereas John's gospel focuses only on the role of Mary Magdalene, other gospel writers focus on the role that all 3 women played at the tomb of Christ.

In this chapter of **WIB,** I through the leading of the Holy Spirit, quoted scripture from the **Old Testament** that foretold of Christ's crucifixion and resurrection. And from the New Testament, I quoted from the gospel writers actual eyewitness accounts of Christ's death and resurrection.

My prayer is that God will enlighten the readers of this book to the *exponentially improbability* (impossibility) of these prophesies of the Old Testament being actually fulfilled in the New Testament--concerning Christ crucifixion and resurrection--without the involvement and will of the hand of a Supernatural, Omnipotent and Omniscience God.

My prayer is that the readers of this book will believe, ascent and hearken to the truth I have relayed in this chapter: **"In order to be a Christian, one must believe that Christ was crucified and rose from the dead."**

A CHRISTIAN MUST ACCEPT AND BELIEVE IN THE CLEANSING, FORGIVING, REDEEMING AND PROTECTING POWER OF THE BLOOD OF CHRIST

In order to be a Christian, one must accept and believe in the cleansing, forgiving, redeeming and protecting Power of the Blood of Christ.

The book of Hebrews teaches us *that without the shedding of blood there is no remission of sin.* That is why in the Old Testament God commanded the Hebrew children through his prophet Moses to bring animals such as sheep, bullocks, rams, pigeon doves, goats and others which HE considered as *clean*, to the Temple, so that the priests could offer them up as spiritual sacrifices before the Lord and shed and sprinkle **blood** upon the altar, the **Mercy Seat** and upon other *holy things* in the temple, to appease the wrath of God and atone for the sins of the Offerers. God hates sin; *and* evil cannot tarry in His sight. Therefore, when *fallen man* comes unto God's presence, he must come with **blood**.When Adam and Eve committed *royal treason* and *disobedience* against God in the Garden of Eden, spiritual darkness fell upon them and they became spiritually blind, and could not, on their own accord, find their way back to the **SPIRIT of Light**. Jehovah Jireh, seeing them in this dark and direful condition, came down from the portals of heaven to provide them a way back unto His glorious and luminous presence.

In an attempt to relieve their shame and rid themselves of their horrid sin, which had occurred because of their treasonous act, Adam and Eve covered themselves with fig leaves. But the leaves of the tree could not cover their spiritual nakedness and shame or rid them of their sin. As I stated earlier in this chapter and it is reiterated throughout Scripture: **Without the shedding of blood there is no remission of sin**.

<u>**Something**</u> or <u>**Someone**</u> will always have to die to pay the death penalty which sin requires. So when **Jehovah Jireh** *stepped down* into the garden in the cool of the day, He had to kill an animal and shed its blood to provide covering and atonement for Adam and his bride.

I wrote, pertaining to this topic in my book **The Power Of Love,** these words: "...The cure for the disease of sin was one that could only be administered individually. Every boy and girl that came into the world through Adam and Eve loins would have to go to Jesus, the *Great Physician*, to receive the cure for themselves...The cure was costly,

Over time, the cure would cost the lives of millions and millions of animals through daily sacrifices on the altar of repentance. But the blood of those innocent animals would only momentarily safeguard and shield *repentant man*, in his filthy garments from the wrath and judgment of a Holy and Just God. Under the Old Testament, once yearly, the High Priest would cautiously enter behind the purple veil of the **Holy of Holies** to offer up unto God a special annual blood sacrifice. This too was only a temporary fix for sin. The Hebrew children had other offerings and rituals they performed, to gain favor with God but all of their sacrifices were only a *shadow* and a *type* (read Exodus, Deuteronomy and Leviticus). It would take more than the blood of animals. The blood of animals could not permanently abate God's wrath and judgment, or satisfy as a permanent propitiation for **man's** sin. **Animal blood was only a temporary fix.** The ultimate sacrifice and price that would have to be paid for man's **sin-cure** would be the ***Blood of Jesus,*** God's Only Begotten Son. On a rugged wooded cross, atop the hill of Calvary, outside the gates of Jerusalem, our Lord Jesus Christ would purchase our **sin-cure** and redeem us back unto Himself, by suffering and shedding His Own precious Blood... ***The Son of God had to die.*** *God so loved the world, He gave His only begotten Son so that whosoever believed on Him would not perish but have everlasting life."*

In our contemporary churches today, we do not preach and teach on the importance and value of the blood of Christ as the Saints did in formal years. Preachers, poets and gospel writers of *yore*, would preach, write and sing of the significance and power of the blood of Christ with joy unspeakable and full of glory; realizing that only the **Blood** can *cleanse, save* and *make a sinner whole* and protect him from the **Evil One.** The older Hymnal books are filled with **Blood songs.**

It was Christ's blood, which made it plausible and possible for sinful man to come boldly before the throne of God and seek help in time of trouble...Only the blood of Christ could abolish the enmity and tear down the wall of iniquity which sin had erected between man and God. Without *the shedding of Blood*, there is no hope for man's forgiveness, eternal redemption and salvation...*there is only the certainty of hell and death.*

What can wash away my sin? Nothing but the blood of Jesus. **What can make me whole again?** Nothing but the blood. *"And I heard a loud voice saying in heaven, Now is come salvation, and strength, and the kingdom of our God, and the power of his Christ: for the accuser of our brethren is cast down, which accused them before our God day and night. **And they overcame him by the blood of the Lamb**, and **by the word of their testimony**; and they loved not their lives unto the death."* (Revelation 12:10, 11)

Salvation, *protection*, *strength* and the *power* of the Kingdom of God *are all* woven, compacted, and centered in the blood of Christ. The **Accuser Himself** cannot break through the blood-barrier to destroy the servants of God or bereft them of their rights, when they, covered by the BLOOD, obey God's commandments and faithfully proclaim God's word. *"And they overcame him by the blood of the Lamb, and by the word of their testimony."* Even if God allows the Destroyer to destroy the **body** of a blood-bought believer, the Blood of the Lamb will faithfully cover and eternally protect the **soul** and **spirit** of that saint.

A great example of the protecting power of the blood of God is illustrated in the book of Exodus. In this book, the Egyptians had held the people of God in bondage for over four hundred years; until God Himself grew weary and commanded His servant Moses to tell Pharaoh to let His people go. He gave Pharaoh nine chances to comply with His command but each time, Pharaoh hardened his heart and would not comply. Finally God initiated a tenth and final plague. He sent Moses to warn Pharaoh that if he did not let His people go that He (God) would destroy the first-born son of every occupant of Egypt. Pharaoh yet would not comply.

God then sent Moses with instruction for His people. *"Then Moses called for all the elders of Israel, and said unto them, draw out and take you a lamb according to your families, and kill the Passover. And ye shall take a bunch of hyssop, and dip it in the blood that is in the basin, and strike the lintel and the two side posts with the blood that is in the basin; and none of you shall go out at the door of his house until the morning. For the Lord will pass through to smite the Egyptians; and when he seeth the blood upon the lintel, and on the two side posts, the Lord will pass over the door, and will not suffer the destroyer to come in unto your houses to smite you."* (Exodus 12:21-23)

That night, when God sent the destroyer (Death Angel) into Egypt to destroy--all of the first-born sons of the Egyptian, were killed by the Angel of Death, as, the Ever-Presence God, stood by and watched. But none of the Hebrew children were destroyed *became* the blood of the lamb painted upon the lintel and the doorposts of their modest dwelling shielded and protected them. When the Death Angel saw the blood, the Ever-presence God commanded him to by-pass that domain. **Thank God for the blood!!! Thank God for the BLOOD!!! Hallelujah!!!**

In the New Testament, when Christ was beaten beyond recognition and nails pierced His hands and feet and a spear His side...and a bloody crown of thorns adorn his skull and *ripple of flesh* hung from His bloody back, it was for our redemption and atonement. *He was wounded for our transgressions and He was bruised for our iniquities.*

Just as the High Priest, in **The Old Testament**, went behind the purple veil of the **Holy of Holies** once a year, bearing the blood of animals for the covering of his people sin, Jesus, after being crucified and rising from the dead, would carry His own precious blood before the thorn of His Father and would present it before the heavenly **Mercy Seat** as an eternal sacrifice--not only for the covering of sin but for the eternal remission, forgiveness and cleansing of the sin of the Believer.

Hebrews puts it this way: *"And almost all things are by the law purged with blood; and without shedding of blood is no remission. It was therefore necessary that the patterns of things in the heaven should be purified with these; but the heavenly things themselves with better sacrifices than these. For Christ is not entered into the holy places made with hands, which are the figures of the true; but into heaven itself, now to appear in the presence of God for us; Nor yet that he should offer himself often, as the High Priest entereth into the holy place every year with blood of others; For then must he often have suffered since the foundation of the world; but now once in the end of the world hath he appeared to put away sin by the sacrifice of himself."* (Hebrews 10:22-26)

When Christ shed His precious blood on Calvary and presented it before the Mercy Seat of God in heaven, He dealt sin its final blow. Now, being forgiven, cleansed and covered by the Blood of Christ, we as saints of God can come before His throne boldly having our sin- purged....clothed in the Righteousness of God.

I wrote this chapter to remind my readers of the *power* and *significance* of the blood of Christ. Buddha's, Mohammad's, and all the blood and teachings of *every founder* of *every religion* on earth—both past and present, cannot wash away sin...Neither do they dare make the claim. Only the Blood of Christ, God's only Begotten Son, can cleanse man or his sin and securely bring him unto the eternal and peaceful presence of his Creator and God.

I pray, that having read this chapter, you too will know and agree that: **In order to be a Christian, one must accept and believe in the Cleansing, Forgiving, Redeeming and protecting power of the Blood of Christ.**

A CHRISTIAN MUST BELIEVE IN A LITERAL HEAVEN AND HELL

In order to be a Christian, one must believe in a literal heaven and hell. But first, before we go any further, let us consider and answer the following question:

Is there life after death?

Many of my readers will say **<u>yes</u>** to this question…but a few will say **<u>no</u>**.

Those, such as **atheists**; whom will say **<u>no</u>**, believe that when a person physically dies, all consciousness and memory dies with that man, woman or child and *that* man, woman or child remains eternally in the grave; *knowing nothing* and *void of* soulical and cognitive *existence*…eternally void of will, thought and emotions.

But others (such as **religious folks** and **agnostics**) will either *believe in* or *think about* some type of life after death. Of this group, a number of them will conclude that everyone, after their physical demise, will go to heaven and as in a **child's fairy tale**, live happily ever after. The remainder of this group believes that there is a Judgment after death for the actions and behavior of **men** and that *the good and the evil* **men** do on earth will be rewarded or punished accordingly… Thus, Evil

Doers will suffer future *lost and penalties* but morally honest and good men will gain *favor and rewards*.

In order to be a Christian, one must believe in *some type* of life after death because the **bible** teaches us that, ***there is***. But what does the bible teaches us about the after-life? What should Christians believe?

THIS! *"…It is appointed unto man once to die, but after this the judgment:"* (Hebrews 10:27)

The bible teaches us that there is a literal heaven and a literal hell and those who do not except Jesus, as Lord and Savior in this life, will find themselves **j-u-d-g-e-d** and cast into hell and the Lake of Fire after their physical demise. But fortunately, on the other hand, **there is good news!!!** The bible also teaches us that those who accept Jesus Christ as Lord and Savior in this life *will*, after their death be *judged* and *rewarded* everlasting life with the Holy Trinity (**Father, Son** and **Holy Spirit)** in the *new heaven* and *new earth*.

Like God, man is also a **triune being:** man consists of **body**, **soul** and **spirit**. Thessalonians 5:23 states, *"And the very God of peace sanctify you wholly; and I pray God your whole spirit and soul and body be preserved blameless unto the coming of our Lord Jesus Christ."*

We see man in his *triune form* even from his **formation**: *"And the Lord God formed man of the **dust of the ground** and breathed into his nostrils **the breath of life**; and man became a **living soul**."* (Genesis 2:7)

The **body** of man is from elements of the earth or the *dust of the ground.* The **spirit** of man is from the **Eternal**

Living Spirit or **Breath of God**. The **spirit** is the life force in man that connects man to the spiritual world and allows man to live, breathe and exist on the earth-plane. The **soul** is the *fundamental essence* of man—consisting of **mind**, **will**, and **emotions**. The **soul** is who man is: **man is a soul.**

Many charismatic Christians believe that man is a **spirit** who has a **soul** and lives in a **body**. I do not believe this. Like, the late Bishop G. E. Patterson (former presiding bishop of the International C.O.G.I.C. church) and many other notable theologians; I believe that man is a **soul** who has a **spirit** and lives in a **body**. The bible teaches and affirms this. But to believe that man is fundamentally a **spirit** who has a **soul** and lives in a **body** is not a *doctrinal error* that will cause one to go to hell or lose his or her salvation...but it is a *teaching* that will have men focusing-on and seeking solely after spiritual development and growth, when saints should be, through prayer and *by the grace and word of God*, seeking to develop and renew their mind by allowing the *mind of Christ* in them to rule and lead them to total submission to the **Holy Spirit;** by mentally obeying and hearkening to *their perfected born-again spirit man.*

When God saved us, He created in us a clean heart and gave us a *perfect born-again spirit*. Spiritually wise, we became complete—spiritually whole and lacking nothing. It is our soul (mind, will and emotions) that now needs change: **renewal** *and* **transformation**. In the *born-again spirit* of a believer, the fruit of *love, joy, peace, longsuffering, gentleness, goodness, meekness, temperance* and *faith* exist and dwell in its totality. The complete package of the fruit of the Spirit and God's enabling virtue and grace, which allows men and women to live a holy and victorious life, arrive in the hearts of men and women the very moment they accept Christ as Savior and Lord and become born again. But the believer's **mind**, **will** and **emotions** must be daily transformed and developed before the believer can fully walk in the Spirit and exemplify and manifest the fruit of righteousness. Paul told the Corinthians, *"For though we walk in the flesh; we do not war after the flesh: (For the weapons of our warfare are not carnal, but mighty through God to the pulling down of strong holds;) Casting down imaginations, and every high thing that exalteth itself against the knowledge of God, and bringing into captivity every thought to the obedience of Christ."* (II Corinthians 10:3-5) In the above text, Paul informed the Corinthians that the devil's warfare and attacks against them was not specifically a warfare against their *flesh* or *carnal man*—but it was a warfare against their **soul** (mind, will and emotions) Therefore, Paul instructed the Corinthians that *in order* to win the battle, it would be mandatory and necessary for them to control their thoughts and imaginations by meditating upon, obeying and speaking *and* proclaiming the *mighty* **Word of God**.

When Paul says, *"...the weapons of our warfare are not carnal..."* many preachers and believers instantly assume that our **weaponries of warfare** are *spiritual*. They are to an extent...but Paul was referring to warfare *or* battle that takes place and can only be fought and won, through the grace of

God, by casting down ungodly imaginations and thoughts on the *soulical* battlefield of the *mind*.

In Romans chapter 12, verses one and two, Paul pleads and begs us in capital letters, **to do this:** *"I BESEECH you therefore brethren, by the mercies of God, that ye present your bodies a living sacrifice, holy, acceptable unto God, which is your reasonable service. And be not conformed to this world; but* be ye transformed by the renewing of your mind, that ye may prove what is that good and acceptable and perfect, will of God."* **God's perfect and divine will for us as saints, is for us to renew our minds through prayer, the study of the Word, fasting, and through daily physical practice of obedience to biblical principles and concepts.**

Later on, Paul tells the Philippians from his prison cell in Rome to do this: *"If there be therefore any consolation in Christ, if any comfort of love, if any fellowship of the spirit, any bowels and mercies, Fulfil ye my joy, that ye be likeminded, having the same love, being of one accord, of one mind...Let this mind be in you, which was also in Christ Jesus."* (**Philippians 2:1, 2, 5**) As Christian, we have the mind of Christ; and to be successful followers, we must allow the mind of Christ to rule and operate in our soul.

Man is fundamentally a soul who has a God-given life **producing spirit** and he lives in a **body**. Man's basic essence and makeup is **soul**. The **soul** is what makes him **Man** and gives him *uniqueness* and *individuality*. The **body**, consisting of elements of the earth, is the only temporal part of man. The **soul** and **spirit** of man are everlasting—they are eternal.

They will exist forever. After physical death, the spirit of all men returns to God but the soul will spend its eternity in either heaven or hell.

Solomon taught in his sermon, Ecclesiastes chapter 12 and verses 6 through 7, that when a man dies, whether that man is *saved* or *not* that that man's spirit returns unto the Lord who gave it. *"Or ever the silver cord be loosed, or the golden bowl be broken, or the pitcher be broken at the fountain, or the wheel broken at the cistern. Then shall the dust return to the earth as it was: and the spirit shall return unto God who gave it."*

When the body is ravaged with sickness or physically damaged beyond human repair, the **spirit** and the **soul** exist the **body**. The spirit returns to God, who originally loaned it to man so he could live in the earth; and the soul goes either to heaven or hell. Let's read and listen to part of a story Jesus records of two men deaths and observe what happened to them. *"And it came to pass that (Lazarus) the beggar died, and was carried by the angels into Abraham's bosom: the rich man (Dives) also died, and was buried; And in hell he lift up his eyes, being in torments..."* (Luke 16:22-23a)

In the above text, Jesus tells the story of two men who departed this life, Lazarus and Dives. One man's soul goes instantly to Paradise or Abraham's bosom. But unfortunately, the uncaring and Godless rich man, lifted up his eyes in hell.

Jesus said in Matthew chapter 10 and verse 28: *"And fear not them which kill the **body**, but are not able to kill the **soul**: but rather fear him which is able to destroy both **soul** and **body** in hell."*

The bible doesn't say that the spirit that sinneth shall surely die. It warns us that the *soul that sinneth it shall die...* Man is a soul. *"Behold, all souls are mine; as the soul of the father, so also the soul of the son is mine:* **the soul that sinneth, it shall die.**" (Ezekiel 18:4). Death for a soul is eternal isolation and speration from the Spirit of God.

By examining Scripture, line upon line, precept upon precept, here a little and there a little, this is what I believe: **I believe and I'm assured that man is a <u>soul</u> who has a <u>spirit</u>** (the essence and breath of the life of God) **and lives in a <u>body</u>.**

When a man who has accepted Christ dies and Christ precious blood has atoned for his sin, that man's spirit and soul as one-entity returns to God. Eventually, at the sound of the trumpet, when the believer's body is raised incorruptibly from the dead, the believer will then joyfully and eternally exist in the **Creator's** presence in his triune form; as a **body, soul** and **spirit** *being.*

If a man does not accept Christ as his Lord and Savior, and dies without repentance, that man's spirit (life giving force from God) will return to the God who gave it and that man's soul, separated from the Life and Spirit of God, will find itself *in hell,* awaiting his body, which on the day of judgment will also be cast into *hell and the Lake Of Fire.*

"And I saw a great white throne, and him that sat on it, from whose face the earth and the heaven fled away; and there was found no place for them. And I saw the dead, small and great, stand before God; and the books were opened: and another book

was opened, which is the book of life: and the dead were judged out of those things which were written in the books, according to their works.

And the sea gave up the dead which were in it; and death and hell delivered up the dead which were in them: **and they were judged every man according to their works.** *And death and hell were cast into the lake of fire. This is the second death.* **And whosoever was not found written in the book of life was cast into the lake of fire.**" (Revelation 20:11-15)

Just as there is eternal judgment and damnation for those who do not except the Lord Jesus Christ as their savior, there is also eternal life and joy for those who do except Him as Savior and Lord. The Apostle Paul teaches us in II Corinthians, chapter five, verses six through nine that to be *absent from the body* for a believer *is to be present with the Lord.* Therefore, when a believer in Christ dies, as the **body** goes to the grave to be resurrected later, the **soul** and **spirit** of that believer goes directly to heaven to be with the Lord.

In John, chapter fourteen, verses one through three, Jesus prepares and consoles His disciples with these words as He informed them of His soon earthly departure: "*Let not your heart be troubled: ye believe in God, believe also in me. In my Father's house are many mansions: if it were not so I would have told you. I go to prepare a place for you. And if I go and prepare a place for you; I will come again, and receive you unto myself; that where I am, there ye may be also.*"

For about 2000 years now, Jesus has been working on a mansion or abode in heaven for His believers. He has been preparing a glorious and splendid place to receive His Beloved Church and Bride. John observed and recorded this in the book of Revelation: *"And I saw a new heaven and a new earth: for the first heaven and the first earth were passed away; and there was no more sea. And I John saw the holy city, New Jerusalem, coming down from God out of heaven, prepared as a bride adorned for her husband. And I heard a great voice out of heaven saying, Behold, the tabernacle of God is with men, and he will dwell with them, and they shall be his people, and God himself shall be with them, and be their God. And God shall wipe away all tears from their eyes; and there shall be no more death, neither sorrow, nor crying, neither shall there be any more pain: for the former things are passed away."* (Revelation 21:1-4)

In order to be a Christian, one must believe in a literal and physical heaven and hell. I hope the scriptures I have given you from God's word in this chapter of my book, **WIB**, have encouraged and prompted your heart to believe and prepare for the **Day of Judgment**.

Jesus is coming back soon for a church without spot wrinkle or blemish…a glorious church that has been washed and cleansed by the blood of the Lamb. Christ is coming back for a people of faith who trusts Him and is working, praying and watching for His appearing.

We're living in the last days. And many today, have been beguiled by the devil *to believe* that there are many ways to God and to heaven.

God anointed and assigned me to write this book to warn you that there is only one name given among men whereby we must be saved and that name is JESUS (Acts 4:12) Proverbs, chapter fourteen and verse twelve admonishes us that, *"There is a way which seemeth right unto a man, but the end thereof are the ways of death."*

Jesus said in John 14:6, *"...I am the way, the truth, and the life: no man cometh unto the Father, but by me."* I will end this book with Jesus' own words: *"Then said Jesus unto them again, Verily, verily, I say unto you, I am the door of the sheep. All that ever came before me are thieves and robbers: but the sheep did not hear them. I am the door: by me if any man enter in, he shall be saved, and shall go in and out, and find pasture. The thief cometh not, but for to steal, and to kill, and to destroy: I am come that they might have life, and that they might have it more abundantly."* (John 10:7-9)

P.S. If you have any questions are inquiries concerning this book, feel free to email me. Author: rlshepherdjr@yahoo.com

I'll be happy to hear from you and I'll gladly respond to your questions and inquiries.

CPSIA information can be obtained
at www.ICGtesting.com
Printed in the USA
BVHW070919151020
591022BV00002B/191